THE
Southerner's
HANDBOOK

HARPER WAVE

An Imprint of HarperCollins*Publishers*
www.harperwave.com

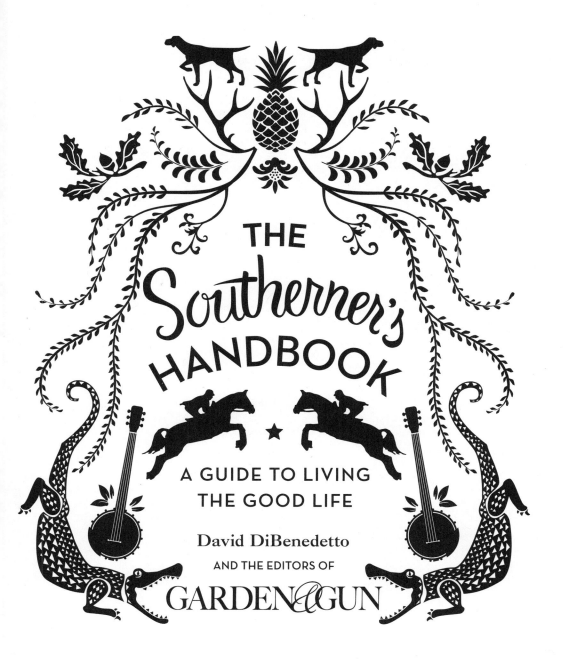

THE Southerner's HANDBOOK

A GUIDE TO LIVING THE GOOD LIFE

David DiBenedetto
AND THE EDITORS OF

GARDEN&GUN

HarperCollins books may be purchased for educational, business, or sales promotional use. For information, please e-mail the Special Markets Department at SPsales@harpercollins.com.

FIRST EDITION

Illustrations by Bruce Hutchison
Designed by Jennifer Heuer

Library of Congress Cataloging-in-Publication Data has been applied for.

ISBN 978-0-06-224238-9

13 14 15 16 17   OV/RRD   10 9 8 7 6 5

BECAUSE I WAS BORN IN THE SOUTH, I'M A SOUTHERNER. IF I HAD BEEN BORN IN THE NORTH, THE WEST, OR THE CENTRAL PLAINS, I WOULD BE JUST A HUMAN BEING.

—*Clyde Edgerton*

CONTENTS

Part Two: STYLE / 49

Part Three: DRINK / 89

Part Four: SPORTING & ADVENTURE / 127

Part Five: HOME & GARDEN / 183

Part Six: ARTS & CULTURE / 223

INTRODUCTION:
MY SOUTHERN EDUCATION

I HAVE A CONFESSION TO MAKE. I DON'T MAKE GOOD BISCUITS. AND I'M A PRETTY POOR SHOT IN A DOVE FIELD. THESE ARE JUST A COUPLE OF THE SOUTHERN SKILLS I'M FAR FROM PROFICIENT AT. THEY WERE NOT PART OF MY UPBRINGING.

Though I was born and raised in Savannah, Georgia, my parents were decidedly not Southern, both having grown up in Brooklyn, New York. But my surroundings most certainly were. Our house sat on a tidal river flanked by a sliver of marsh. A small jon boat and a rusty outboard motor delivered me deep into some of the most beautiful landscapes in the Lowcountry—all teeming with fish, birds, the occasional alligator, and enough submerged oyster beds to damage an aluminum prop for a lifetime.

My home was also located across the hedge from my Southern mentor, the late William Gerken. He was a retired assistant principal for a local high school, and his wife, Martha, was a grade school teacher. Mr. Gerken was born in Savannah on May 22, 1915, putting him on a perfect trajectory for World War II. He served in the navy but saw little action, save for one day on an air patrol when the crew spotted an enemy submarine off the coast of Florida. The plane circled around and dropped a bomb on what turned out to be not a sub but a rather unlucky whale. Among many of Mr. Gerken's skills was his ability to tell a great story. And the whale story was one of them. Never rushed. Always measured. Meandering with a purpose and then the punch line.

From Mr. Gerken's flat-bottomed wooden bateau, he taught me about the river and the wonders of a tidal creek. At his side, I also learned how to properly clean a flounder, sharpen a knife, pick a flower for a girl, throw a cast net, and plant a vegetable garden.

This was a man who led by example. Up early. Did things right. Went to church on Sundays. Kept an immaculate tool shed. Held the door for his wife. He was always the first to welcome new neighbors to the street. In fact, he was sort of a neighborhood sage.

On one unforgettable occasion, I discovered a large tick that had latched onto my nether regions. My mother prudently dragged me next door, where my six-year-old frame was plopped on Mr. Gerken's dining room table, and he unceremoniously removed the bugger before I knew it.

Mr. Gerken also knew that the natural world was full of signposts if you cared to read them. When the dogwoods bloomed in the spring, the whiting would be running thick in the river. And a full-moon night in September meant the largest shrimp of the year would be leaving the marsh en masse on the falling tide, making it a perfect time to fill the bottom of the jon boat with dinner.

At eighteen, I left for college in Vermont and then later moved to New York City to follow my dream of becoming a magazine editor. And while I was grinding away on those late nights, I would often remember what Mr. Gerken would tell me when I griped about some onerous task I had to complete. "Butter Bean," he would say, "hard work ain't easy."

These days I'm back in Dixie and at the helm of *Garden & Gun*, a magazine that represents all that I love about the South. Now my Southern education is further bolstered by the many talented writers—Julia Reed, Allison Glock, Jonathan Miles, T. Edward Nickens, John T. Edge, Guy Martin—whose voices make *G&G* one of the most interesting and surprising reads on the newsstand. If I need a Bloody Mary recipe, I'll dial Julia Reed, who will not only deliver (she prefers a good helping of lime juice) but also pass on a great story about serving Bloodys at a lunch while no one had any idea there was a six-foot chicken snake curled up behind the French doors. The snake was evident in a number of post-party photos. John T. Edge is a must-call before any road trip. His knowledge of culinary pit stops is beyond encyclopedic. (If you're traveling the back roads of South Carolina during the summer, for instance, Edge says you must stop at Dori Sanders's peach stand in Filbert.) When my Boykin spaniel decides she'd rather chase a rabbit than put her nose to the ground and find a quail, I get T. Edward Nickens on the phone for some moral dog support. ("It takes time," he'll say. "And patience.")

We went to all of these great writers and a host of others to help compile *The Southerner's Handbook*. And while you'll find all sorts of wise advice (including the secret to making good biscuits), you'll also find great storytelling. Consider it your own private Southern mentor.

—David DiBenedetto
Editor in Chief
Garden & Gun
Charleston, South Carolina

Part One

FOOD

WHY SOUTHERN FOOD MATTERS (SO MUCH)

BY JOHN T. EDGE

*T*HE REST OF THE COUNTRY HAS LONG WANTED WHAT SOUTH-
ERNERS HAVE. THEY COVET OUR STONE-GROUND GRITS AND
SKILLET-FRIED OKRA. THEY THIRST FOR OUR WHISKEY. THEY WANT
OUR HAM, A CHEF FRIEND ONCE TOLD ME, AS WE LEANED AGAINST HIS
TRUCK, SWIGGING A BOTTLE OF BOURBON. AND THEY WANT OUR HISTORY.

America wants a lot out of Southern food and drink. When Americans go for a
snootful, they reach for Kentucky bourbon. When they seek diversion and abandon,
they travel to New Orleans, our papal city of gastronomy, where brackish gumbos bob
with crab and sausage and Sazeracs brim with rye and bitters.

A supper of braised pork neck bones and pepper-vinegar-spiked collard greens,
served in a cinder-block diner on Atlanta's Auburn Avenue, offers soul-food passage to urban black life. In an age when molecular cuisine is in the vanguard, North
Carolina whole-hog barbecue, pulled from a carcass in vinegar-gilded ropes, offers
a primal answer to pilgrims in search of honesty and authenticity.

As the nation urbanizes, as strip malls, cul-de-sacs, and other nowheres spread,
the South appears the region where farm-to-table eating is a way of life, not a

marketing concept, and food carries the weight of history. At a time when multinationals build pseudo crab shacks and barbecue joints in Walmart parking lots, the South seems a culinary redoubt, where honest cooks stand tall in back-alley kitchens, spearing drumsticks from lard-roiled cast-iron cauldrons. In the midst of an ongoing American nostalgia movement, the South promises the past, preserved in amber, ready to be consumed in the present.

From the 1880s, when Atlanta newspaperman Henry Grady sold the North on a New South, to the 2010s, when every chef and writer in New York City seems to take a summer road trip to New Orleans in search of the secret to the fried chicken at Willie Mae's Scotch House, Southern foods and Southern cooks have captured the attention of outlanders—and insiders like me.

Born in Georgia, in the home of a Confederate brigadier general, I began grade school during the last days of the civil rights movement, as Martin Luther King, Jr., refocused his efforts on feeding our less fortunate brothers and sisters. I now live and work in Mississippi, the state that birthed novelist William Faulkner. My son plays in the pasture where Faulkner gamboled as a boy, and my wife cooks weekday dinners of salmon croquettes, following the recipe on the back of the can, just as the Nobel laureate did.

I love my region. Deeply. I'm proud of what our people have wrought, despite and because of our peculiar history. I balance that love, however, with questions. About who we are and how we got here. About who cooks, who cleans, and who gets to take a seat at the welcome table.

To glean answers to those questions, I've sipped iced tea with former Klansmen and present-day civil rights leaders. I've eaten cheeseburgers and fried okra with an Elvis impersonator. I've talked harvest techniques with a black man who converted his farmland from pesticide-dependent tobacco to organic heirloom collards. I've talked animal husbandry with a white man who tried to convince the rest of the region that possum was the next other white meat.

During those conversations, I learned

that food offers entrée to talk of big-picture issues. Like race and class, gender and justice. Through the years, when I tried to tackle those matters head-on, I often lost an audience. But at tables piled high with country ham, buttermilk biscuits, and redeye gravy, I've marveled as all have leaned in close to eat, to talk, to listen. I've come to believe that time at table offers our best chance for all—for black and white, rich and poor—to acknowledge our past and celebrate our future in a spirit of reconciliation.

In a region bound by a tragic past, we Southerners find common purpose in shared creations. Like music. Like art. Like food. In a region where our relationships to various symbols have long been problematic, our beloved provincial dishes—from pulled-pork barbecue to fried chicken drizzled with honey, from hoppin' John capped with chow-chow to blue-crab gumbo thickened with dried sassafras—serve as unifying totems of people and place.

Our relationship to food is complicated here. Agriculture is one of the reasons people left the region during the Great Migration of the early and mid-twentieth century. For many poor whites and blacks of previous generations, farm life meant toil, poverty, and penury. Now our agricultural legacies and the strength of our honest farm-to-table bonds are drawing people back to the region.

The South was once the nation's number-one economic problem. Families went without food. Babies from Appalachia and the Delta, with distended bellies and listless eyes, were television poster children for the Great Society poverty initiatives of the 1960s. Now the South is the nation's number-one obesity problem. And many families, raised on a diet of double-crust freezer-case pizzas, take in too much of the wrong kind of food.

Our attitudes about Southern foodways are not static. Like all expressions of culture, they evolve.

Insiders and outsiders alike long dismissed Southern food as grits, greens, and grease. "Southern cooking has been perverted by slatterns with a greasy skillet," wrote Atlantan Ralph McGill back in the 1940s. Singer Bette Midler once told a Charleston, South Carolina, audience in the 1980s that grits tasted like "buttered kitty litter." And both were, to a certain degree, right.

Southern cookery went off the tracks for a while. We bought into the faster-cheaper-better industrial-food mantra. We ditched lard-frizzled wedges of cornbread in favor of slices of bagged white bread with the texture of a wasp nest. We quit putting up our own summer peaches and began buying canned freestones from the West Coast.

But a correction is afoot. A slow and steady return to the old ways and the old truths, filtered through new imperatives. Over the past several decades, writers like Virginia's Edna Lewis and Tennessee's John Egerton, along with chefs like Alabama's Frank Stitt and North Carolina's Ben Barker, have shaped a New Southern Cuisine, reliant on local farmers and artisans, dependent on traditional methods and practices, reflective of all contributors to the canon, especially the peoples of African descent who previously got short shrift.

Southern food has emerged as our pan-national cuisine. Hipsters from Brooklyn now descend on our mountain precincts in search of chocolate gravy, an Appalachian dish now falling out of favor in Kentucky, where it was once a Saturday-morning standard. Hippies from Berkeley now go questing for the last fish muddle in eastern North Carolina, hoping against hope to meet the old codger who still cooks his onions down in rendered salt pork. Emboldened by the views of outlanders, Southerners have begun to see the value in their own cookery, to comprehend that polenta is just grits with a mellifluous Italian accent.

After a long fallow period, the South is reclaiming its culinary heritage, paying down debts of pleasure that have accrued over generations. We now celebrate the pit masters who have long stoked our fires and flipped our hogs. We now honor the farmers who began saving our seeds long before we began referring to certain vegetables as heirlooms.

Southern food, as we know it today, is the potlikker and pone of enslaved

Africans and their progeny. It's the ham-shawled guinea hen of plantation gentry and their country-club dynasts. It's the cracker-topped and canned-soup-thickened casserole served by working-class cooks and their sires. It's the okra-threaded gumbo, once stirred in back-of-town cottages by Creoles of color, now served by white-toqued chefs in tony restaurants.

The state of the Southern Food Nation is good. Our cookery is vital and progressive. Our best meals, our most rewarding times at table, lie ahead.

CAST-IRON CARE

ACROSS THE SOUTH, one piece of cookware reigns supreme: the almighty cast-iron skillet, so good at conducting and distributing heat that you can bake, braise, sear, fry, stew, or roast in it with equal success. Walk into any Southern kitchen, and you'll often find one front and center on the stove. But if you're new to cast iron, don't overlook one essential step: Before you get cooking, you've got to season it.

Seasoning a skillet has nothing to do with spices. Because the surface of a new cast-iron skillet is porous, fat has to be baked into those crevices, filling them up to make a smooth cooking surface—a natural version of the modern "nonstick" pan. Most instructions these days recommend seasoning a new skillet with vegetable oil, which can leave a gummy film. Purists prefer a more traditional method. "The only tried-and-true way to season a cast-iron skillet is with lard," says Southern-food historian John Martin Taylor, author of *Hoppin' John's Lowcountry Cooking* and *The New Southern Cook.*

With its gorgeous shiny-black patina, a properly seasoned cast-iron skillet is durable enough to last several lifetimes. Taylor owns skillets handed down from his mother and grandmothers. "Both of my grandmothers, from either end of Tennessee—McNairy County on the Tennessee River and Sevier County in Appalachia—cooked every day in cast iron," he says. "Mind you, these women could not have been more different. The South is a big place, and there are hundreds of miles and hundreds of years of diverging histories between folks in the Mississippi Delta and those in the Smokies. Tennessee is *long*, but cast iron is one common denominator."

SKILLET SEASONING

1. WASH a new skillet with warm soapy water once to remove the thin coating of wax applied at the factory. That's the last time you should ever wash it with soap.

2. HAVE the butcher grind enough fresh pork fat to nearly fill the skillet. Place a thin layer of water (about ⅛ inch) in the bottom, and then add the fat. Put the skillet in the oven set to 225 degrees or on top of the stove over very low heat.

3. MELT the fat slowly; it can take an hour or more. When the solid matter (called cracklings) turns brown and sinks to the bottom, strain the fat into a glass jar with a tight-fitting lid and wipe out the skillet. After the fat has cooled, cover it and store in the refrigerator. You now have rendered lard for biscuits and piecrusts—and a seasoned skillet.

4. AFTER each use, rub the inside of the skillet with bacon grease and wipe out the excess. The salt in the bacon grease will help preserve the skillet and keep food from sticking to the surface. If you must wash it to remove any dust or bits of burned food, don't even think about putting it in the dishwasher. Use only cold water and a natural-bristle brush, then dry it thoroughly and wipe down with bacon grease.

PERFECT FRIED CHICKEN

OF ALL THE CLASSIC Southern foodstuffs—beloved through generations for their down-home preparation and sheer deliciousness—fried chicken has suffered the most at the hands of the homogenizing chains, which long ago ran off with Great-Grandma's tasty yard-birds and twisted them into bland, crust-armored Cluckensteins.

The secrets to giving this most exemplary of soul foods some actual soul don't have anything to do with a certain Kentucky colonel or a magic number of herbs and spices. They have to do with a few old-fashioned details and time-proven techniques. "Making great fried chicken is really pretty simple," says Raleigh, North Carolina, chef Ashley Christensen, owner of Beasley's Chicken + Honey, where the birds are done right, and the difference is nothing short of inspiring.

First, find the highest-quality chicken you can and brine it overnight in a solution of salt and sugar, which helps infuse moisture and flavor. A minimal buttermilk-and-flour coating will also let the chicken's natural flavor come through, as will frying it in neutral canola oil. For a perfect crust, the classic method is to shake the brined and buttermilk-drenched chicken in a paper bag full of salted flour. A cast-iron skillet is the only way to fry, but don't drown your chicken; use just enough oil to come halfway up the sides of the skillet, keeping the oil at 325 degrees, which will cook the meat all the way through while the crust turns golden brown. Armed with Christensen's tips and recipe, you'll be turning out perfect—and perfectly simple—fried chicken in no time.

ASHLEY CHRISTENSEN'S
FRIED CHICKEN

1 **whole chicken,** cut into pieces
8 cups cold **water**
1 cup **granulated sugar**
1½ cups + 1 tsp. **kosher salt**
1 gallon **ice cubes**
Canola oil as needed
4 cups **all-purpose flour**
4 cups **whole buttermilk**

TO BRINE the chicken, bring the water to a boil, add the sugar and 1½ cups salt, stir until dissolved, and remove from heat. Combine the brine and ice in a large food-safe container. Place the chicken in the brine, cover, and refrigerate for at least 10 hours and no longer than 12 hours.

FILL A large cast-iron skillet with just enough canola oil to come halfway up the sides; heat to 325 degrees. Meanwhile, fill a paper grocery bag with the flour and the remaining teaspoon of salt, fold closed, and shake to combine. Fill a large bowl with the buttermilk. Remove the chicken from the brine and pat each piece dry. Dip the pieces in the buttermilk, let the excess drip off, and place in the bag with the flour mixture one by one. Fold the bag closed and shake to thoroughly coat each piece of chicken. Shake off excess flour and lay your chicken in the skillet. Adjust the heat as necessary to keep the oil at 325 degrees. Fry, turning only once, until fully cooked: interior at 165 degrees.

LOVE YA, HONEY

WITH OUR DIVERSE FLORA and geography giving precious honeybees the raw material for creating fine art, the South is home to some of the finest honey anywhere. And Southerners have taken advantage of this fortunate circumstance for a very long time. Biscuits with butter and honey? Bliss. Grits with a touch of honey? Folks do it all the time, and they're not crazy. And don't forget glazing roast birds, pigs, and so on.

True Southern honeys bear little resemblance to the generic sugary sap sold in plastic bears at grocery stores. "Commercial honey is often blended, and there is no clear, distinct flavor," says Walter Bundy, executive chef of Lemaire in Richmond, Virginia's Jefferson Hotel, who has installed bee colonies on the hotel's roof. "Most local honey will be from one floral source, and much like wine, the nectar's flavor is determined by soil, geography, climate, and weather."

Fresh honey should be plentiful at Southern farmers' markets from April through fall. Look for raw, unpasteurized honey that's "monofloral," such as these outstanding varieties. They put those plastic bears to shame.

SOURWOOD HONEY: Rarely sold beyond the Blue Ridge and Allegheny Mountains, this highly prized honey comes from the skinny, soaring Appalachian Lily tree, which blooms late June through July. The honey is most frequently described as "indescribable," a tribute to its floral sweetness and complex gingerbread flavors.

TUPELO HONEY: The name "tupelo" gets slapped on honeys across Florida, but true tupelo honey can be traced back to small stands of Ogeechee tupelo trees along the Apalachicola and Ochlockonee Rivers. In order to fix up their bees with the right trees during the short spring blossoming season, tupelo producers sometimes keep hives on secluded docks in forbidding swamps. The honey smells like pears and tastes like cotton candy.

BLACK LOCUST HONEY: The Southern cousin of the European acacia honey that commonly turns up on cheese plates, black locust is an eagerly awaited springtime honey in North Carolina and Georgia. Although much of the harvest is mixed with tulip poplar honey, pure black locust honey is delicate, fruity, and startlingly clear.

ORANGE BLOSSOM HONEY: The same trees responsible for the South's most popular citrus fruits provide the nectar for orange blossom honey, a vigorously sweet honey produced in Florida and Texas.

GALLBERRY HONEY: Gallberry trees grow as far north as Nova Scotia, but their honey-giving properties are acknowledged almost exclusively in Georgia and Florida. Thick Gallberry honey, esteemed for its golden hue and lack of granulation, is especially suitable for baking.

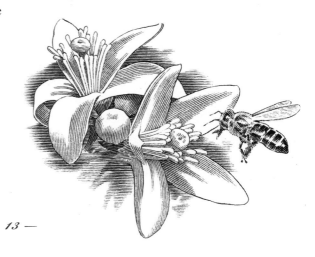

BIG BAD BUTTERMILK BISCUITS

BY CHEF JOHN CURRENCE

MAKING GREAT Southern-style biscuits is about understanding and respecting the science behind them. It's about the right balance of fat to flour, and a deft hand at combining and kneading them. When it comes to the fat, I like a combination of butter and lard in my biscuits. Lard brings a flavor and crispiness that no other fat lends, while butter brings the leavening and its own flavor.

Butter is composed of three basic elements: butterfat, milk solids, and water. Oddly enough, water is about the most important part of this equation. Biscuit recipes typically read, "Cut butter into flour mix until mix resembles a coarse meal." The reason for this is that you want the fat to remain intact, in its original form, while being broken into as many

small bits as you can get. Biscuits don't require a lot of kneading once the dough comes together, because, again, you want the butter to remain as intact as it can. When biscuits cook, each one of those tiny little butter bits breaks down inside a pocket of dough, and that little bit of water boils and creates a pocket of air after the steam escapes into the biscuit itself.

It wasn't until I understood what was at work that I made good biscuits. I labored over them and was meticulous in my technique and execution. I was convinced the old-fashioned approach was the only way to make biscuits come out exactly how I wanted them. Then legendary Charleston, South Carolina, chef Louis Osteen ended up in our restaurant kitchen one morning. He saw us toiling over our biscuits and asked why we weren't cutting the flour in with a food processor. (We were making about five hundred biscuits.) He shoved us out of the way and showed us how to quickly cut the fat in by pulsing the ingredients in the food processor. That blessing of technique by the Pope of Things Southern was all we needed. We now use it to make thousands of biscuits weekly at our restaurant Big Bad Breakfast, and it makes whipping up great biscuits at home a lot easier too.

BIG BAD BREAKFAST
BUTTERMILK BISCUITS

(Makes about 15 biscuits)

1½ oz. **butter**
2 oz. **lard**
2 cups **flour**
½ tbsp. **baking powder**
1 tsp. **baking soda**
1 tsp. **salt**
½ tsp. **black pepper**
1 tbsp. **sugar**
1 cup **buttermilk**

CUT BUTTER and lard into small cubes and place in freezer on a pie tin or plate. Mix dry ingredients in a food processor. Turn machine off, and add butter and lard to dry mix, distributing evenly. Using metal or dough blade, pulse until mix resembles a coarse meal. (Alternatively, you can cut the fat into the dough with a pair of knives.) Dump this crumble into a stainless steel bowl and slowly drizzle in buttermilk while stirring with a fork. This mix should not quite come together into a ball.

FLOUR YOUR hands and begin turning dough in the bowl and mashing with the heel of your palm until it begins to come together. As soon as it does, turn out onto a floured surface. Flatten and fold the dough repeatedly (no more than six or eight times) until it becomes even in moisture and somewhat smooth. Roll out to three-quarters-inch thickness. Cut dough into rounds and bake on a dry baking sheet at 400 degrees for 12 to 15 minutes or until golden brown.

SUPREME SAUSAGE GRAVY

NOTHING CROWNS a beautiful Southern biscuit better than the gravy conjured up out of the grease and crumbles of some spicy pork breakfast sausage. Sure, have a patty or two with your eggs, but leave the rest for the gravy. This is wisdom.

Food lore traces this countrified staple back to Appalachian logging camps—you'll sometimes hear the term *sawmill gravy*—and it will forever be regarded as a classic Southern workingman's breakfast: hearty, tasty, and inexpensive, made to feed a mess of laborers. In some parts of the South, a split biscuit with sausage gravy is still referred to as "poor-do," which speaks to its economy, and "life everlasting," testimony to its staying power.

If you'd like to eat like those old lumberjacks but with a touch of sophistication, you might want to hunt up chef David Bull. Bull has made his name cooking at such fine Texas eating establishments as Congress in Austin, but he's embraced the soulful dish as part of his culinary signature. "I've put biscuits and sausage gravy on the menu everywhere I've worked," he says. "It's warm and comforting but also unexpected."

Traditionalists will find it easy to spot Chef Bull's refinements. Heavy cream enriches the white gravy, while fresh, aromatic sage leaves bring out the best in the pork breakfast sausage, topped off with a fried sage leaf garnish that takes the dish from belly warmer to showstopper.

DAVID BULL'S SAUSAGE GRAVY

2 tbsp. **unsalted butter**

1 small **yellow onion,** peeled and diced (about ½ cup)

1 tbsp. finely chopped **fresh sage leaves**

2 tbsp. **flour**

¼ lb. **pork breakfast sausage** (not links), fried and crumbled

2 cups **half-and-half**

2 cups **heavy cream**

¼ tsp. **cayenne pepper**

Salt to taste

Lemon juice to taste

Tabasco to taste

Worcestershire to taste

IN A large saucepot over medium heat, melt butter until almost foamy. Add the onion and cook until it appears translucent, about 2 to 3 minutes. Add the sage, stirring frequently. Do not brown. Quickly stir in flour. Add the sausage, half-and-half, and heavy cream, and bring sauce to a boil. Lower heat and simmer until liquid is slightly thickened, about 10 minutes. (Adjust the heat so it doesn't simmer over the sides.) Add cayenne pepper and season with salt, lemon juice, Tabasco, and Worcestershire to taste.

FRIED SAGE GARNISH

Vegetable oil (enough to "float" the leaves)

6–8 **sage leaves**

Salt to taste

HEAT THE oil in a heavy-gauge saucepot with tall sides over medium heat until it reaches 325 degrees. Carefully drop each sage leaf into the hot oil and turn once after 30 seconds. Cook until color darkens, about 15 to 20 seconds more, and remove leaves from oil. Place on a paper towel to drain. Season with salt.

SPLIT YOUR biscuits in half by hand to make a lumpy bed for the gravy, then lightly spread with butter and toast until warmed. Place your toasted halves in the center of a shallow bowl, dollop on your sausage gravy, and garnish with the fried sage.

GREAT GRITS

PITY PRETTY MUCH the entire rest of the world: They just don't seem to get grits. But don't judge too harshly. The "quick" or "instant" (and rather tasteless) varieties that have become ubiquitous these days bear only a passing resemblance to a good bowl of ground hominy and certainly don't do any favors for converting the skeptical. No one knows that better than chef Sean Brock, a Virginia native whose work at Husk and McCrady's, his Charleston, South Carolina, restaurants, has made him a revered figure in the Southern food world and beyond.

"I could eat grits every single day," Brock says. "When I travel, no matter where I go, the first thing I do when I come home is eat a bowl of grits. That brings me back." A stoveside purist who insists on the freshest, most local ingredients, Brock brings to grits the passion of a Southern gourmand and the expertise and cosmopolitan tool kit of a thoroughly modern chef. His rules for grits begin at the source. "Each region has its own variety of corn," he says, "and to me, that's what you should be cooking." Grits milled nearby come fresher and imbued with local flavor. If you can't buy local, Brock suggests Anson Mills as a good backup. And to preserve freshness, keep your grits in the freezer.

To get the most out of that flavor, a little preparation is in order. Soak your fresh-milled grits overnight before cooking, three parts water or stock to one part grits. "If we're doing a dish with onions," Brock says, "we might use a vegetable stock with a little more onion. If we're pairing with a chicken dish, we might use chicken stock."

But water's fine, too. The idea is to soften the grits so they cook faster, which helps preserve both texture and flavor.

The next day, skim off any bits of floating chaff and transfer the mix to a pot. Bring it to a boil, then reduce the heat and stir for seven to ten minutes, or until the starch takes hold. "You'll see it," Brock says. "You'll be stirring water and grits, and all of a sudden it locks." Now put the lid on your pot and take the heat down to a simmer, stirring the grits every seven or so minutes. Keep water or stock warm on the stove to add as necessary. (If a spoon can stand straight up in the grits, they need more liquid.) While cooking times vary, soaked grits should be ready in about an hour.

Brock believes in keeping the seasoning simple. Halfway through the cooking process, he adds salt—just a teaspoon or so for every cup of dry grits—and a pinch of white pepper. Once the grits are finished, he also mixes a good spoonful of butter into the pot for a smoother, creamier texture. When making cheese grits—"there is a time and a place," he says—Brock favors a mild cheddar, like the hoop cheddar that thickened his grits growing up. Just don't overdo it. Grate the cheese on top of your grits for a layer of molten dairy that supplements but doesn't overwhelm.

GRITS BY MAIL

If you can't find quality grits near your home, try one of these three suppliers.

ANSON MILLS, COLUMBIA, SOUTH CAROLINA

Chefs all over the country swear by the flavorful grits that farmer and culinary historian Glenn Roberts mills from heirloom corn the old-fashioned way—on wheels of South Carolina granite.
www.ansonmills.com

GEECHIE BOY MARKET AND MILL, EDISTO ISLAND, SOUTH CAROLINA

On a farm just an hour outside of Charleston, the shrimp-and-grits capital of the world, Greg Johnsman grinds some of the tastiest grits in the Lowcountry.
www.geechieboymill.com

MILLS FARM, ATHENS, GEORGIA

Tim and Alice Mills named their signature Red Mule Grits, featured at several big-name Georgia restaurants, after the 1,250-pound mule that powers their gristmill.
www.redmulegrits.us

THE ULTIMATE APPETIZER

IF THERE'S ONE DISH you'll find doubled or tripled up on at a Southern party spread, whether potluck or planned, it's deviled eggs. And even then, the folks who brought them aren't likely to be leaving with any leftovers. The "devil" part? It's not because they're a source of temptation (though they are); it refers to the spices that add that nice piquant kick.

Southern cooks have lately taken to dressing up their eggs with various accoutrements—country ham, chilled Gulf shrimp, poached tomatoes. But connoisseurs will rightly tell you that what matters most is the springiness of the white and the tang of the yolk. To please the fussiest of them, start with eggs a few days removed from the nest, since fresh eggs are frustratingly dodgy come peeling time. Put the eggs in a pot, cover with an inch or so of cool water, and boil. Once the water's sputtering, reduce the heat to a low simmer and cook for eight minutes. To avoid overcooking the yolk, shock the eggs in an ice-water bath for thirty seconds before peeling. Slice the eggs lengthwise and remove the yolks.

If the boiling process is a science, doctoring up the yolks is an art. But if you're short a treasured yellowed recipe card with handwritten instructions for the absolute perfect proportions of mustard to mayonnaise, not to worry. Just combine a dozen yolks with a half cup of your favorite mayo and a quarter cup of your favorite mustard, then add salt, pepper, and paprika to taste and you'll have a preparation worth handing down.

If you like your eggs creamier, you might add a bit of butter. If you like your eggs spicier, a few dashes of Tabasco or grated horseradish will do the trick. And there are plenty of folks who won't declare deviled-egg filling ready until they've added a teaspoon of lemon juice and a tablespoon of pickle relish. But by then you're just tinkering with perfection.

WHERE THERE'S SMOKE . . .

FORGET RELIGION or politics. If you want to start an argument in the South, just bring up barbecue. Beef versus pork, whole hog versus shoulders, the proper style of sauce: When it comes to barbecue, everything is controversial.

There's a reason for that. Barbecue stirs Southern passions like no other food, and it's been doing it for a very long time.

The roots of barbecue in the South stretch back to the early colonial days, when English settlers adopted from Native Americans both a method of cooking meat and the word used to describe it. The local tribes, Robert Beverley noted in his *History and Present State of Virginia* (1705), roasted meat by "laying it upon sticks raised upon forks at some distance above the live coals . . . this they, and we also from them, call barbecuing."

Outdoor barbecues featuring whole hogs, rum, and dancing were an indispensable part of colonial Virginia social life. Settlers carried the institution with them as they made their way from Virginia down into the Carolinas and Georgia and eventually over the Appalachians into Tennessee and Kentucky and along the Gulf coast all the way to Texas. Barbecues were the preeminent way that antebellum Southern communities celebrated the Fourth of July, complete with speeches, music, and toasting. Massive barbecues drew thousands of people together to hear political candidates speak, to raise money to build railroads, and to celebrate important civic events.

Around the turn of the twentieth century, barbecue transitioned from something served at large outdoor public get-togethers into a product of commerce. Experienced cooks began selling smoked meats from impromptu stands, and those stands evolved into permanent barbecue restaurants with brick and cinder-block pits instead of trenches dug in the ground.

Those early restaurants were where the now-famous regional barbecue variations were born, as pit masters settled on one or two types of meat to serve, standardized a few regular side dishes, and formulated their own sauce recipes. An informal apprenticeship system helped codify the style of a particular city or region, as young people went to work at established restaurants, learned the technique and style of their barbecue mentors, then branched out to open their own places.

Those old-school barbecue joints and the variety they engendered are why barbecue lovers today argue so passionately over what "real barbecue" is. And while any attempt to put bounds around such a concept is sure to provoke howls of protest from partisan camps, most Southerners' definition would at least include these common elements: large cuts of meat cooked low and slow over hardwood coals. From there it devolves into a fog of opinion: Does it have to be a particular type of meat? Be cooked directly over the coals or smoked over indirect heat? Served with a sauce or dry?

The answer, of course, is that real barbecue mostly comes down to whatever style you grew up with, the version that reminds you of home and evokes memories of family gatherings. For centuries, barbecue has been bringing people together throughout the South, and it's still doing that today. It's a matter not just of the stomach but of the heart, too.

Naturally, composing a list of recommended barbecue stops is as perilous as defining what real barbecue is. But if you're in search of authentic tradition and the splendid variety of Southern 'cue, the following five long-standing joints are great places to start.

SCOTT'S BAR-B-QUE

HEMINGWAY, SOUTH CAROLINA

The secret to Rodney Scott's barbecue, he will tell you, is that it's made with "a whole lot of love." It also doesn't hurt that he and his crew cut and chop their own wood, reduce it to coals in a burn barrel, and use it to cook whole hogs on massive cinder-block pits, mopping them again and again with a peppery vinegar sauce. Scott's is a throwback to country stores that sold barbecue as a sideline business, though these days it sells far more slow-cooked pork than it does canned goods or loaves of bread.

PAYNE'S ORIGINAL BAR-B-QUE

MEMPHIS, TENNESSEE

The claim that the barbecue pork sandwich was invented in Memphis rests on shaky foundations, but there are few better places to sample one than at Payne's. The menu is the same as when it opened in 1972, featuring slow-cooked pork shoulders and ribs and, of course, a legendary barbecue sandwich. It's big and sloppy, a hamburger bun loaded with chopped pork with generous crispy outside bits. The pork is topped with tangy, spicy red barbecue sauce and a scoop of bright yellow mustard–tinged coleslaw.

WILBER'S BARBECUE

GOLDSBORO, NORTH CAROLINA

In 1962, Wilber Shirley opened his restaurant on Highway 70 in Goldsboro, and today it stands as one of the premier examples of the eastern North Carolina style. In the brick cookhouse out back, he and his team cook whole hogs over oak in closed pits. The meat is coarsely chopped and served on a platter or on a sandwich, accompanied by a spicy vinegar-based sauce. Don't forget a bowl of Brunswick stew. Red, tomatoey, and loaded with corn and potatoes, it's a classic North Carolina side dish.

LEXINGTON BARBECUE #1

Lexington is the undisputed capital of Piedmont North Carolina–style barbecue, and Lexington Barbecue #1 is as good as any of the town's twenty or so barbecue restaurants. Wayne Monk learned the craft from legendary barbecue mentor Warner Stamey, and that means he doesn't cook the whole pig, just the shoulders, and he does it over hickory and oak. The pork is chopped fine and served with a tomato-tinged vinegar-based sauce. That same sauce is used to dress the fine-chopped barbecue coleslaw, which, along with crisp hush puppies and a couple of dill pickle slices, composes a classic Piedmont North Carolina barbecue plate.

SMITTY'S MARKET

Edgar A. "Smitty" Schmidt purchased Kreuz Market in 1948, and today his daughter, Nina Sells, and grandson, John Fullilove, run the business in the same building where the Kreuz family started smoking meat more than a century ago. Fullilove cooks briskets, pork ribs, pork chops, coarse-ground sausage, and even prime rib over seasoned post oak. It's sold by the pound, sliced to order, and wrapped in brown butcher paper with a couple of slices of white bread and traditional extras like onions and pickles. These days, they'll give you a bottle of sauce if you ask for it, but, really, why would you want to?

BOIL YOUR GOOBERS

BOILING PEANUTS IS ONE of those Southern things that just seem downright kooky to folks more familiar with the dry-roasted ball-game snack. But boiling "goober peas" is as storied a Southern ritual and social occasion as a catfish fry or a pig picking—and the legumes themselves, thus prepared, are right up there with okra and collard greens in the South's culinary pantheon.

Like so much of the region's gastronomic heritage, boiling peanuts was probably brought over from Africa centuries ago. Historically, fresh raw peanuts—not dried, like those used for roasting—were used, and that's still preferred among some purists. But people often boil dried peanuts as well, since the raw window closes quickly on the heels of harvesting. The idea is to take naturally flavorful peanuts, still in the shell, and boil them in salt water to soften everything and make it all more savory. Eating them is akin to slurping down oysters, brine and all. But if you're still dubious, consider this: If they weren't so good, you wouldn't find private goober patches dotting the Southern countryside or see busy roadside stands selling bags hand over fist.

"What's so beautiful about boiling peanuts is that anyone can do it," says Matt Lee. "It's as simple as putting the right peanuts in the right water for a long time." In addition to authoring award-winning Southern cookbooks, Matt and his brother, Ted, have sold the South

Carolina specialty since 1994 through their Lee Bros. Boiled Peanuts Catalogue, which offers the obvious as well as other Southern staples, like fig preserves and stone-ground grits. Here's the brothers' take on how to do it yourself.

THE NUT: "You can use fresh green peanuts or dried peanuts. Eight out of ten times, people use dried, often of the Valencia variety, which is sweeter than the fresh Virginia peanut. And dried peanuts are available year-round. The Virginia peanut, which you can find in the late summer and fall, is softer and more delicate. A little grassier."

THE WATER: "For salty, South Carolina–style peanuts, the water should have about the salinity of seawater. In fact, we tried using seawater this past summer and it works great. Otherwise, start with one cup of salt per two gallons of water and correct to taste as you boil."

THE BOIL: "How long you boil depends on the peanuts—whether they're thick, thin, wet, dry. Typically, green peanuts are ready in two to three hours, and dried peanuts in six to eight, but you should sample frequently while boiling and take them out when you feel like they're ready."

MIND OVER MOLLUSK

THAT AN AVERAGE OYSTER holds itself shut with a little more than twenty pounds of pressure ranks pretty high on the list of useless facts—unless you're the poor shucker on the other end of the oyster knife. But rest easy: There are a few tricks to help you get to the briny goodness inside with a minimum of tussle.

As owner and bar master at Eddy Teach's Raw Bar, on Florida's St. George Island, James Frost shucks around fifty dozen oysters a day and has learned the hard way that it's a matter of technique. How long did it take him to perfect his skills? "About two years, maybe seventeen stitches, more than a hundred knives, and more oysters than I can count," he says.

The first thing to know, Frost advises, is that if you're exerting a lot of force,

you're doing something wrong. The secret to shucking a raw oyster isn't about brute force; it's about leverage. And having the right tools, namely a good oyster knife and glove. The glove goes on the hand that holds the oyster (your nondominant hand) primarily to protect against the shell's sharp edges.

At the oyster's hinge (the pointy end), there is usually a small opening where the two halves of the shell have grown slightly apart from each other. This is the spot to wedge in the tip of your knife. From here, it's all in the twist. "A lot of times people will overdo it," Frost says. "They'll wiggle up and down and try to force it. Just twist your wrist. That will provide enough leverage for the rear of the upper shell to come loose."

All that's left is cutting the muscle that connects the meat to the shell and, hardest of all, deciding whether you want it with lemon juice, hot sauce, or nothing but the sublime liquor nature has provided.

OYSTER SHUCKING 101

1. HOLD the oyster right side up—meaning the cupped side is facing down—in a gloved hand, and work the tip of the knife into the hinge, where the top and bottom halves of the shell meet at the narrow end of the oyster. Twist your wrist, using the blade as a lever to pop the two halves of the shell apart.

2. ONCE the shell is loose, slide the knife blade along the inside hollow of the top shell to sever the adductor muscle. Be careful not to spill the liquor. Discard the top shell.

3. BEFORE serving or slurping, slide the knife underneath the oyster meat to cut it loose from the bottom.

OKRA, MEET SKILLET

MOST SOUTHERN gardeners can tell you a few things about okra: It has big, lobed leaves and pretty yellowish flowers with red or purple eyes, and it produces seedpods that are the heart and soul of gumbo. What most probably don't know is that it's also one of the healthiest fruits in the Southern larder, rich in vitamin C, folate, and antioxidants, with plenty of calcium and potassium, too. It probably came to the South with Africans in the early eighteenth century, and folks took to it immediately. Thomas Jefferson had most likely been munching on the stuff for decades before he became POTUS.

But for all its benefits and staying power, the slender okra may carry the heaviest burden of all Southern garden staples. There's no way to put this delicately: The stuff is just naturally slimy.

Luckily okra has an ally in the frying pan, since heat prompts the plant's mucilage—so handy as a gumbo thickener, so unappetizing to eaters with low goo tolerances—to quickly go from oozy to firm. If that sounds a little more appealing, batter up.

Combine one cup of yellow cornmeal with one-quarter cup of flour, seasoning to taste with salt, pepper, and cayenne. Then cut the pods into half-inch segments, dip them in buttermilk, and dredge them through the cornmeal mix while heating just enough bacon fat in a cast-iron skillet. When the fat's very hot, add the okra. Once you're seeing golden brown, fetch the okra out with a slotted spoon, and serve straightaway with your favorite hot sauce or a nice vinegar-pepper sauce.

KNOW YOUR BARBECUE SAUCES

THE ESSENCE of barbecue might be composed of meat, wood, and smoke, but the vast majority of barbecue joints (good ones anyway) lend almost equal significance to the sauce, and there are as many variations as there are hairs on a pig's hide. Still, nearly all of them can be put into one of five primary categories by their base condiments: ketchup, ketchup-vinegar, vinegar, mustard, and mayonnaise. (The absence of sauce is also a key part of certain barbecue traditions, especially in Texas.) Sauces are associated with particular regions of the South, and allegiances run fierce. Here then, the why and wherefore of the leading styles.

HEAVY TOMATO: For barbecue novices, heavy tomato sauce *is* barbecue sauce, thanks mostly to the marketing efforts of food conglomerates, which have stocked the nation's groceries with bottles of thick reddish-brown sauces. But homemade versions still predominate in the Delta, and particularly around Memphis, where pulled-pork sandwiches as well as ribs and spaghetti are soaked with sweet acidic sauces made from ketchup, cider vinegar, and brown sugar or molasses.

WHITE: Perhaps the most geographically limited of all the major sauce styles, white sauce sounds like a practical joke to those who haven't eaten barbecue in northern Alabama. It's sometimes thick, sometimes thin, sometimes ivory, and sometimes as white as a fresh sheet of paper, but it's always made with mayonnaise. Legendary pit master Big Bob Gibson developed the sauce back in 1925 to complement his chicken, but it's sometimes paired with other kinds of smoked meats too.

MUSTARD: South Carolina's colonial governors urged Germans to settle in their territory, believing they'd bring stability and sophisticated farming techniques to the frontier. But immigrants also brought their love of mustard, and the golden sauce served in the state's midsection pays tribute to a heritage of plates piled high with pork sausages. Made with mustard, vinegar, sugar, and hot sauce or cayenne, it's typically tangy and subtly sweet.

LIGHT TOMATO: North Carolinians love to squabble about politics and college basketball, but sauce talk can get especially heated. Eaters in eastern North Carolina believe adding ketchup to a vinegar sauce is heretical. Proponents of Lexington-style barbecue

to the west believe otherwise. Light tomato sauces, also served in Georgia and South Carolina, became popular around the turn of the last century, when bottled ketchup emerged as the nation's top condiment. Don't tell an eastern North Carolinian, but the ketchup's sweetness counterbalances the acridity of strong smoke.

VINEGAR-PEPPER: Vinegar-pepper sauce is the fountain pen of the sauce cabinet: simple, elegant, and pedigreed. A throwback to the earliest days of barbecue, when coastal settlers dressed their smoked hogs with homely blends of vinegar and hot red peppers, this thin, tart sauce still reigns in the eastern Carolinas and western Kentucky. Sauces have become flashier since vinegar-pepper served as the nation's standard, but acolytes would argue they haven't gotten any better.

WILD FOR RAMPS

IN THE UPLANDS of the South, they're called ramps, but you may have heard them referred to as wild leeks, which they are, or spring onions, which they also are. But it's ramps around here, and we've been making dishes tastier with them since the Native Americans showed us how. To get some idea of the pre-European popularity of this magical and pungent vegetable, which has the distinction of smelling like garlic but tasting like strong onions, look no farther than the Windy City. Chicago was named after a bunch of ramps growing near Lake Michigan. The natives called the plant *shikaakwa*, which some French naturalist recorded as *chicagou*.

That said, there's still no place ramps are more popular than in the South. But first, you've got to find them.

Allan Benton, whose old-fashioned country hams and smoked bacon command respect at white-tablecloth eateries all over the country, has spent decades foraging for the garlicky plants in his native Appalachia. "We go to the mountains for ramps during the month of April," he says. "That's when the leaves come out of the ground—three flat leaves." When warmer weather arrives, in early May, those leaves shrivel up and drop off.

Benton looks for ramps at elevations of 3,000 to 5,000 feet. Although there's no telling where you might find ramps growing, he has good luck near mountain creeks. "It's often a dead giveaway if I can find a small branch of a creek coming down the mountain. Early in the season, when the foliage hasn't come in at high elevations, you can stand on the mountain and look down the side. If you see a green area, that's ramps."

Benton heads to the mountains with a portable stove, a sack of potatoes, unsmoked bacon (as ramp tradition dictates), and some company, and at the end of a hunt, the party settles in for a meal. The potatoes, cubed, cook in a skillet with the bacon while Benton washes, dices, and adds the ramps, that amazing aroma filling the mountain air soon afterward. "I've had some real delicacies in some fine restaurants," he says, "but nothing is as satisfying as those ramps and potatoes cooked in bacon grease on a spring day."

TOP-SECRET FISH BATTER

WHETHER A FISH comes from the ocean or a mountain stream, it's vulnerable to being ruined by a saggy, soggy coat of inferior fry. If it's light and crisp you're chasing, you'll need a proper batter, which is just two ingredients more complicated than the cornmeal and salt finish that's long reigned in Delta juke joints and North Carolina fish camps.

While that basic coating's fine for very delicate fish, here's a trick for frying many firm white fish—such as catfish and grouper—you'll find across the South, usually in red plastic baskets with some fries.

Try mixing equal parts flour and very cold club soda—or a good ale, if you're feeling festive. Either way, the carbonation aerates and lightens the batter. Add one cup of each to a bowl with two teaspoons of baking powder and a pinch of salt, and get to dipping. Skip the oft-endorsed preliminary run through a stand-alone mound of flour, which only serves to make the finished product distastefully thick, and dip the fish directly into your top-secret mix. Fry up in a cast-iron skillet with peanut oil—or lard, if you're game—until golden, light, and crisp.

ESSENTIAL SOUTHERN COOKBOOKS

SOUTHERNERS HOLD tightly to old favorites, especially when food is involved. So while plenty of good cookbooks have hit store shelves in the past couple of decades, it's the worn-out copies of the classics that we tend to treasure most. These five books are among the most vital and influential in the Southern culinary canon.

The Virginia House-wife

BY MARY RANDOLPH (1824)

The foundational text of Southern cooking, this book was the work of one Mary Randolph, a famed cook and hostess in Richmond, Virginia. Within its pages, fried oysters and cornbread share space with colonial holdovers like molasses beer and roast calf's head. Also present: the first written recipe for macaroni and cheese.

Charleston Receipts

COLLECTED BY THE JUNIOR
LEAGUE OF CHARLESTON (1950)

The oldest Junior League cookbook still in print, *Receipts* contains 750 recipes culled from the old families of Charleston, South Carolina, in the years following World War II. With dishes that trace Charleston's history from the first days of settlement to the cocktail-party era, this cookbook sums up centuries of Southern coastal life.

The Taste of
Country Cooking

BY EDNA LEWIS (1976)

Born in Freetown, Virginia, Edna Lewis moved to New York City during the Great Depression. While in the city, she found fame cooking at Café Nicholson, which became a hangout for the city's bohemian crowd. But it was with this book, a portrait of her rural childhood replete with recipes and stories, that she found her voice as a champion of fresh, local Southern cuisine.

The Foxfire Book of
Appalachian Cookery

EDITED BY LINDA GARLAND PAGE

AND ELIOT WIGGINTON (1984)

Ever wonder how to dress a squirrel, or how to make rhubarb wine? Or would you like to try something more familiar, like an apple stack cake or a sheet of baking powder biscuits? From pokeweed to pickles, this culinary distillation of the popular Foxfire series covers the ins and outs of eating in Appalachia with more than five hundred as-told-to recipes from a collection of mountain cooks.

Southern Food:
At Home, on the Road,
in History

BY JOHN EGERTON (1987)

The founder of the Southern Foodways Alliance, John Egerton gets down to the very roots of Southern cooking in this hybrid of a travel guide, encyclopedia, and cookbook. Then he follows them upward, speaking with modern-day chefs, academics, and eaters. All told, it remains the ultimate big-picture survey of Southern food past and present.

DO-IT-YOURSELF CHARCOAL

SCOTT'S BAR-B-QUE IS based out of an old tin-roofed variety store on the fringes of Hemingway, South Carolina (see page 24). It's a popular lunch spot for locals, but it's also a destination for food lovers from all over the world, drawn to Scott's by praise from major-league chefs and barbecue junkies. An old-school practitioner of whole-hog barbecue, pit master Rodney Scott makes his coals from local hardwoods. Here's how.

1. START WITH LOGS: "I use pecan, hickory, and oak. Pecan gives meat a nutty flavor. Hickory adds that classic, smoky, 'outside' flavor. Oak and hickory together create a flavor that's indescribable. There's something about the two that just makes great barbecue."

2. BUILD YOUR FIRE: "I have an old steel drum with the top cut off, a doorway cut out of the bottom, and a truck axle in the middle that holds the burning logs. To get the wood going, we put a little paper on top of the axle, under the logs, and then light a wad of paper beneath it. Within an hour or so, we have coals. I keep my logs stacked high so I can use fresh-cut wood, because the burning wood on the bottom dries the stuff at the top of the stack."

3. SHOVEL OUT THE COALS: "The wood is going to break down into little pieces of ember and charcoal. You take those as soon as they drop and put them under your pig, your steak, your turkey. If you're doing a pig, you're going to be doing that for at least twelve hours. If

you're doing turkey, three or four hours. We usually shovel every ten or fifteen minutes, but it's a touchy-feely kind of thing. You just have to keep the rotation going, because once those coals go out, they're just ash."

GOOD WOODS

To the uninitiated, wood is wood. But the experienced pit master knows that different types of trees make different types of barbecue. Hickory, oak, and pecan work wonders in smokers across the South, but here are three more woods that bring big flavor to pork butts, briskets, and other smoked meats.

APPLE: Fruitwood coals infuse meat with bright, fresh-from-the-orchard flavor. And while you'll find people in different parts of the country using everything from persimmon to guava, apple is a straight-down-the-line selection that works equally well with beef, pork, poultry, and fish.

CITRUS: Maybe it's because citrus trees are few and far between in barbecue meccas like North Carolina and the Texas Hill Country, but you'll rarely see orange, lemon, or grapefruit woods in a pit master's pile. That's not because they don't make for delicious barbecue. The wood burns down into coals that impart a sweet and tangy flavor.

MESQUITE: Mesquite is to smoking wood what mustard is to barbecue sauce. Some 'cue lovers swear by it, and others wouldn't touch it with a ten-foot hickory log. But the two sides can agree on one thing: It is powerful stuff. Many pit masters choose to use the hot-burning wood in concert with milder options like pecan and oak.

QUEEN CREOLE'S ROUX

AS THE BASE FOR all manner of Southern gumbos, gravies, sauces, and stews, roux is as elemental as bacon in many kitchens across Dixie. It first appeared in the South in places like New Orleans and Charleston, South Carolina, via the French, who base three of their grand culinary tradition's "mother" sauces on roux: béchamel, velouté, and espagnole. A good roux is deceptively simple—it's just flour and fat—but it's really easy to muck up, requiring know-how and finesse to nail it.

"To cook food right takes time and love," says Leah Chase, the grande dame of New Orleans Creole cuisine. "I tell people, 'If you're in a hurry, don't even try. Just make your ham sandwich and go.'" Chase has spent more than a half century dishing out gumbo, fried chicken, and other New Orleans staples to crowds at the iconic Dooky Chase's Restaurant. And you'll find few folks who quibble with her roux.

Chase builds hers up with oil when at work, but at home, where she isn't simultaneously simmering gallons of gumbo, she starts off slow, rendering fat from spicy sausage. "If you have sausage, bacon, or anything you can render off, that fat gives your roux extra flavor," she says.

Once Chase has hot fat in the skillet, she adds roughly three heaping tablespoons of flour for every cup of fat. (Many cooks prefer a one-to-one flour-to-fat ratio, but Chase likes a more fluid roux.) She whisks the mixture continuously over medium heat until the flour turns a nutty brown and aromatic, about fifteen minutes. "You've got to stay with it," Chase says. "It's going to stick and burn if you don't." If you begin to see black specks, well, you've burned your roux and it's time to start over.

"The idea is to cook that flour through," Chase says. "Just slow-cook it, so it won't be pasty, without burning it. You'll smell it when it's ready. After that, you add any seasonings and slow-cook it just a little bit longer."

THE SOUTH'S DESSERT

THE ONLY CULTIVATED nut indigenous to the South, the pecan has been used in the region's cooking since the earliest colonists met Native Americans. But the rise of pecan pie—sometimes called Karo pie—came centuries later, commonly traced to a product-based recipe printed on jars of Karo corn syrup, circa 1930.

"That doesn't surprise me," says Hilary White, chef and co-owner of the Hil in Serenbe, a thousand-acre sustainable community located in Georgia's Chattahoochee Hill Country. "There was a day when family favorites were a mix of recipes clipped from the Sunday newspaper and Ladies Auxiliary books. Others came straight off the flour sack."

While pecans grow throughout the South, Georgia has been one of the nation's largest producers since the late nineteenth century. The state's growers even donated enough pecan wood to create the handles for the more than ten thousand torches carried during Atlanta's 1996 Olympics. With peak harvesting months of October to December, it's easy to see why pecan pie became a traditional Southern holiday dessert, and the rich, nutty flavor matches the aromatic spices used in savory Thanksgiving and Christmas recipes. "Every year, my father's parents would drive from Florida to Ohio, where my family lived at the time, stopping in Georgia to buy pecans," says White. "I remember it was dark outside, and we'd sit in the eat-in kitchen, picking them. My grandfather would use the nutcracker, and my grandmother and I would use the nut picks. It was delicate work, because you didn't want to crush the pecans but keep them perfect halves for the pie."

White's maternal grandmother contributed the piecrust, and like most inherited family recipes, it has a few "miracle" ingredients. The flaky tenderness comes from fresh white lard, testament to the recipe's age. And vinegar lends acidity, which enhances the workability of the dough, keeping it so pliable you don't even have to rest it.

"Pie making is sort of a lost art," says White, "and this is a good old recipe." But she did add one more miracle ingredient to her grandparents' version: bourbon. "It has the same flavor nuances of the dark corn syrup and makes the pie even more Southern."

DRUNKEN PECAN PIE

For the piecrust:
(Makes two 9-inch crusts)
1⅔ cups **all-purpose flour** mixed with ¾ tsp. **kosher salt**
⅔ cup **lard**
¾ tsp. **white vinegar**
1 **small egg**
Water

For the filling:
(Makes one 9-inch pie)
¾ cup **granulated sugar**
1½ cups **dark corn syrup**
½ tsp. **kosher salt**
1½ tsp. **all-purpose flour**
3 **large eggs**
1½ tsp. **vanilla**

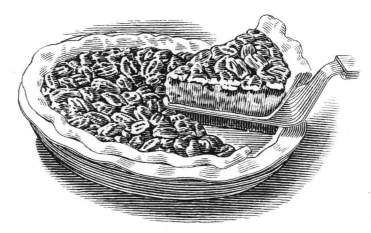

2 tbsp. **bourbon**

1½ tbsp. melted **sweet butter**

1¾ cups **pecans**

TO MAKE THE CRUST: Place flour and salt in a bowl and cut in lard until mixture resembles small peas. In a measuring cup, combine vinegar and egg and add water to make ⅓ cup liquid. Slowly add liquid to the flour mixture, forming dough. Do not overwork. Remove from bowl, halve, and pat into disks. If not using immediately, cover in plastic wrap and chill.

ASSEMBLE THE PIE: Roll out one piecrust disk and fit in a 9-inch pie pan, crimping the edges.

TO MAKE THE FILLING: Combine sugar, syrup, salt, flour, and eggs, mixing well with a hand mixer. Stir in remaining ingredients and pour into unbaked pie shell. Preheat oven to 350 degrees. Bake for 75 minutes (a toothpick inserted in the center should come out relatively clean). Remove and place on cooling rack, allowing the pie to rest for 2 to 3 hours to set properly.

A MESS OF GREENS

A FEW GENERATIONS AGO, most every Southerner knew how to cook collards, the leafy greens that brought many hard-up families through the toughest stretches of the Great Depression. And the best way to prepare a mess of them really hasn't changed, despite modern pleas from nutritionists to bake collards into pasta and stir-fry them with cabbage to protect the vitamins and minerals typically lost during the traditional low boil.

Collard leaves are at their tenderest when they measure about the size of a church fan, but even the smallest leaves require trimming. Once cleaned and sheared of their tough stems, the leaves are ready to waltz with pork, whether in the form of fatback or a few strips of thick bacon. Any bit of smoked swine will do. Cook the meat in a pot or skillet, then add your collards with a little water and cider vinegar, simmering the leaves over low heat until they wilt and fade. Give it time: Collard preparation is typically measured in hours, not minutes.

According to Alex Albright, who chronicled collards for *The New Encyclopedia of Southern Culture*, it's a wise idea to add a whole pecan to the pot because the nut helps to counteract the pungent stench that is the hallmark of collard cooking. Collard lore is chockablock with things that the green is "said to" do: Headache sufferers may press collard leaves to their foreheads, acne sufferers may apply a collard poultice to their blemishes, superstitious types may hang collards over their doorways, and it's a tradition to eat collards on New Year's Day to bring prosperity (the greens represent money).

Once cooked, your collards might enjoy a splash of vinegar or hot sauce or both. They should be served with their own potlikker—the liquid by-product that is your reward for waiting out the long, odoriferous cook—and a wedge of cornbread for sopping.

GO WHOLE HOG

BY JACK HITT

EVEN THOUGH THE slow-food movement can often sound pretentious and artisanal and boutiquey and oh so rococo, it still pisses me off when I go off about the pleasures of slow-cooked hog only to have some twee poindexter roll his eyes and huff some hot air out his blowhole by way of suggesting that he dwells in a Randian free market where his rugged individualism is mighty happy with some franchise-bought pork sandwich and, besides, haven't you lived too long up there in New York with the Yankees and bought into their politically correct propaganda about precious locavorism when the stuff served beneath the well-lit menus at any of the chains found along the miles of Bataan-like sprawl on the way out of town is just as good? And here's the double paradox: If I were to plunge my nine-inch brushed-steel locking tongs straight through this guy's bow tie and into his pencil neck, the law, as it's currently construed, gets me in trouble.

There are just so many things wrong with confusing the pretentious inklings of born-again foodies with the deep pleasure of slow-cooking a whole hog. I try to convert those who casually utter the words "hate to cook" with filibusters about just how easy, even small-*d* democratic, it is to cook a whole hog. Sure it's laborious in the most cathartic sense of that word, but it's not *hard*. Essentially, the heat source is smoke, not hot air, and the meat renders differently. Instead of sizzling the fat—as you do when you put bacon in a pan—you are melting all that interstitial goodness and carrying it through the meat with, depending on your druthers, tasty pecan smoke. There's nothing pretentious in any of that, just lots of awesomeness. To pull this off, you want to put a whole pig on, in my case, some subway grate I bought from a nearby foundry, or any large piece of ungalvanized grill—ungalvanized because you don't want your pig to taste like a fired cap gun, as when licked by a six-year-old boy when nobody's looking, not that there's anything wrong with that.

With the hog on the grill, you want to cover it in some dome-like way (I use cinder blocks and industrial-width tin foil) that creates enough space around the pig to allow for smoke circulation, and then spend eighteen to twenty-four hours shoveling wood cinders—smoldering but never flaming—underneath the pig to maintain a temperature around roughly 200 to 210 degrees Fahrenheit, relying on lots of thermometers from the hardware store (digital, infrared, old-style ice-pick ones), because excessive gear is the American way when it comes to all large-scale backyard enterprises.

A good eighteen-hour pig requires rotating pit crews. For the graveyard shift, I typically rely on bribing a handful of nephews and nieces with a cooler of beer and a guitar. The result the next afternoon is a grand thing that unveils to a yard full of *oohs* and *aahs* every time, because that final hog can, like victory, claim many fathers. The fellowship can't be beat. Don't take my word for it. Here's one of the most revealing entries of any colonial diary, just before the Revolutionary War: "Went in to Alexandria to a barbecue and stayed all Night." That's George Washington writing—our Founding Epicurean, a man who knew how to have a good time and, when he finally got some sleep, founded a nation.

★

Part Two

STYLE

SECRETS OF A SOUTHERN HOSTESS

BY JULIA REED

NCE, IN MY VERY EARLY PARTY-GIVING DAYS, I WAS AGONIZING—ON THE PHONE WITH MY MOTHER—OVER WHAT TO SERVE AT A DINNER PARTY FOR A FAMOUS BOOK CRITIC, A STORIED OP-ED COLUMNIST, AND SOME OF MY COLLEAGUES AT *NEWSWEEK'S* WASHINGTON BUREAU, WHERE I WORKED PART-TIME. ALL THE GUESTS WERE OLDER THAN I WAS AND, CLEARLY, MORE ACCOMPLISHED; I WAS STILL IN COLLEGE, LIVED IN A THREE-ROOM WALK-UP, AND HAD EXACTLY ONE BYLINE TO MY NAME. BUT I COULD COOK, AND FOR WEEKS I'D BEEN CLIPPING RECIPES FROM THE FOOD PAGES OF THE *NEW YORK TIMES*, MOSTLY OVERTHOUGHT AND FAIRLY SOULLESS STUFF UNDER THE HEADING "NOUVELLE CUISINE," WHICH HAD JUST BEEN INVENTED.

Anyway, long distance cost a lot of money back then, and I was driving my mother crazy with a long list of choices that must have sounded pretty terrible because finally she interrupted me and said, "Why don't you just serve something that tastes good?"

I have told this story many times, but it bears repeating because I took it to heart, and almost twenty years later—after I'd served a whole menu of things that tasted good at a party in my Manhattan apartment to a crowd that included an editor from the *New York Times Magazine*—I ended up writing about food for the very paper from which I once cut out all those pompous recipes. The editor who hired me apparently had never seen a pimento cheese sandwich or a deviled egg or a fat piece of rare beef tenderloin on a hot yeast roll until that night, and it impressed him. It impresses most people, which is why my mother's long-ago advice remains my first rule of throwing a good party: The food does not need to be formal or "fancy" or even necessarily expensive to have an impact. In fact, the opposite is usually the case.

For example: Journalist and famed D.C. hostess Sally Quinn tells a story about a night when the caterers screwed up the date of a formal dinner and she had the bright idea to send the babysitter to Popeyes. Chicken and biscuits and red beans and rice were piled into pretty silver, the guests took seconds and thirds and demanded to know the name of the cook, and even the most august cabinet members took off their ties and rolled up their sleeves so as to better get at the good stuff in front of them. Quinn says that her male guests kiss her when she serves mashed potatoes; I get the same response to squash casserole and cheese spoon bread. But this kind of "simple" food takes a certain amount of fearlessness. During my first ever summer in the Hamptons, I was told by the formidable wife of an editor friend that under no circumstances could I serve the pot of seafood gumbo and platters of fried chicken and potato salad I'd planned on having at my debut gathering. "That's not what we do here," she said, instructing me instead to have a seated supper of plain grilled swordfish that was as ubiquitous that summer as shoe leather, and just as tasteless. I was slightly terrified, but I ignored her and I've never seen people so happy. By offering up an exotic (to them) antidote to the asceticism to which they'd unwittingly been subjected weekend after weekend, I set a tone I hadn't even realized I was setting. They drank more and laughed louder, ate the chicken with their fingers, and stayed very, very late (except for the aforementioned arbiter who ostentatiously refused to eat a morsel and left her grateful husband behind when she drove home in a snit).

It was then that I realized that every party should be an antidote—to boring everydayness, to toil and strife, to clean living or the opposite lure of TiVo and takeout Chinese. A good party should enable you to step outside your humdrum existence and into a virtual theater of someone else's creation, a stage set that encourages you to be your best, most hopeful self. And that does not happen when bossy, humorless hosts or hostesses put you on accidental diets or orchestrate the conversation. The two words I feared most during the years I lived in New York City were "table talk." At one point during the meal, a glass would be clinked, and the dread words would be uttered. Each guest was then obliged to offer up his or her opinion on the latest Supreme Court nominee or some equally contentious subject, a forced march that completely shut down all the things that make being around a dinner table worthwhile: witty repartee, serious flirtation, an actual impassioned argument

that ends in good-natured bread pelting rather than oration about the state of the latest immigration bill.

Those table-talk evenings always led me to the nearest post-party saloon where I could have a real conversation and enough booze to get over the previous hours' trauma. Which leads us to the next and most important rule. It is not possible to overbuy the whiskey and wine, and both should be easily accessible from moment one of the event. To that end, there is not a thing wrong with offering people a pre-drink drink, a flute of champagne, say, or a special cocktail mixed up for the occasion and served on a tray (preferably by an actual person) just outside or inside the door. This eliminates any initial stress on the part of your guests and enables festive and well-lubricated passage along the way to the actual bar. If you've got a packed house, make sure you have circulating waiters taking more orders; once at the table, no one should ever have to ask for more wine. By far the most useful gifts my mother ever gave me were a pair of Irish crystal wine decanters that hold almost four bottles apiece. People reach over and refill—a lot—but the wine's still there. It's like the miracle of loaves and fishes but no one sees the magic. Which is the point. Most people don't want to be reminded that they're pounding down a bottle or two of wine all by themselves. They sort of don't want to be reminded that they are drinking at all, rather that they are simply morphing into their most lively and charming and brilliant selves, sort of like Romy and Michele in the high school reunion dream sequence where they look really hot and explain how they invented Post-it notes, complete with the formula for the glue.

But back to the stage set. Outdoor lanterns are always festive; inside, candles are a must. Flowers too, but just as the food should not be too fussy, do not have someone come in and do your house up as if a bride is about to emerge from upstairs on the arm of her father, or worse, someone has died. If you have a yard, use it. My mother has done amazing things in her time with not much more than johnsongrass, and my own favorite trick is to smash grocery store lilies or roses or whatever looks pretty into a collection of julep cups or wine rinsers on the table.

Music is also a must. I once hired a Cajun band whose midget washboard player did backflips across the stage. That definitely got things going, but you could also press into duty your piano-playing best friend (or, in my case, husband) to reinvigorate the after-dinner crowd with a rousing version of "Twist and Shout" or "What'd I Say." There is scarcely a woman alive who does not secretly fancy herself a Raelette, and a generous host or hostess will give her the opportunity.

Finally, if the occasion demands it, have a toast ready, but for God's sake make it funny—and short. At the rehearsal dinner the night before my good friend Anne McGee's first wedding (an occasion she now refers to as "My Big Party"), all the super-serious friends and relations of her Yankee groom went on so long that the bride's brother-in-law passed out at the head table during a recitation of Rudyard Kipling and her uncle finally yelled "Bullshit!" during an especially fawning tribute that made the groom out to be something other than the man-child we knew him to be. The rest of us gave Anne just the right amount of grief in the form of brief musical tributes and suitably hilarious stories that entertained our own selves and (almost) everyone else in attendance.

On the day of the wedding, my parents threw a wedding lunch at which the backyard crowd looked a tiny bit like the Red Sea, featuring the (by now forewarned) Yankees on one side and the rest of us on the other. Not surprisingly, one side stayed later than the other, so that I was late arriving at the bride's house for the ceremony itself. As I slipped inside, I noticed the McGees' good-looking neighbor in front of me wearing a sexy chiffon cocktail dress accentuated by a pair of evening sandals, the straps of which she had tied together and slung over her shoulder. She'd been to a great many of Anne's mother's big parties and well knew the fun she was going to have. Why slow things down later when you can have your dancing feet at the ready? This is hopeful, this is what you aim for, this is the sign of a very good party to come.

THE HARD TRUTH ABOUT COWBOY BOOTS

ALTHOUGH THE LEGEND is regarded as fact in Texas and the story is frequently anthologized, especially in trivia books with titles like *Weird Origins of Normal Stuff*, the modern leather cowboy boot was not designed by Buffalo Bill Cody, and the distinctive pointy-toed look has absolutely nothing to do with the shape of Annie Oakley's breasts, which were, according to historical accounts, as round and mysterious as tumbleweeds. The cowboy boot is a purely utilitarian design created for the working equestrian: Its pointy toe slides easily into stirrups, and the high Cuban heel (which prevents the rider's foot from slipping through) and stovepipe top are both hedges against a terrible death by dragging, should a thrown rider's foot become stuck. These boots were not made for walking.

That said, a good pair of cowboy boots may eventually become as comfortable as a pair of fuzzy slippers, but, as you may recall with a cringe, they do not start out like that. Other than wearing them (and wearing them and wearing them), there are no real tricks to breaking boots or broncos except time, patience, and intestinal fortitude. Risk and commitment are required, so grit your teeth but know that it's worth the discomfort: There's nothing more iconic you can put on your foot. Stiletto heels and oxfords are mere handmaidens.

But about that suffering: To complicate

matters—or possibly because they're sadists—legacy boot makers regard their process as proprietary, so there's not much standardization. Size is relative, and, ever more in the age of online shopping, we *endure* a new pair of boots—and the age-old ritual of scalding pain. We do so believing that, after a period of sweaty, snake-bitten agony in too-snug shoes, boots and wearer will be made one.

Prolonged exposure to water isn't good for leather, but the breaking-in process can, in nearly every case, be sped up by drenching new boots, wearing them until dry, and repeating the process as often as necessary. This will be an extremely uncomfortable experience, teaching the boot pilgrim manifold lessons in long-suffering grace. You will also make sloshing noises when you walk. But don't be deceived: While brutally effective, this is the footwear equivalent of drugging your children. Delicate and exotic skins will never forgive.

For the pain-averse, though, there is another way, a secret long kept hidden by many self-billed tough guys: Buy a size up. That great shame is heaped upon the purchaser of roomy boots is undeniable, but there will be fewer tears—on the outside. And if bigger boots stretch some over their lifetime? Thicker socks.

HOW TO BEHAVE

ALTHOUGH THE PAST FEW decades have taken their toll on standards of propriety all over the country, certain expectations still exist below the Mason-Dixon Line, and they translate quite nicely elsewhere too. To avoid landing in hot water at your next get-together, take a few lessons from Cindy Haygood, of Athens, Georgia's Perfectly Polished, who has sent a whole host of young folks into the world prepared to handle all of the intricacies of Southern etiquette.

It probably goes without saying that any good Southerner must be able to hold a conversation. After all, "people love to talk," Haygood says. But it's important not to make the all-too-common mistake of confusing conversation with monologue.

"You should keep it a give-and-take, a tennis game, a back-and-forth."

If you're keeping up with the news or have just finished a good book, you already have a handful of topics to get the ball rolling. But sometimes in the heat of the moment, that blanking thing happens when coming up with something—*anything*—to say feels darn near impossible. You can try a technique Haygood calls "the conversation alphabet," meaning running through the ABCs in your head for topics that start with each letter. Atlanta? Baseball? Or better yet: Cocktail—and then excuse yourself to the bar.

In the course of conversation, if someone brings up what Haygood calls "the flaming issues"—namely politics, religion, and money—and things start to get uncomfortable, it's perfectly acceptable to change the subject "with a smile on your face and love in your heart."

At an event of any sort, Haygood says, you must always pay close attention to the host. "Follow the host's lead. Never do anything until that person has done it." Seat yourself, take up your silverware, start your meal—and your drink, even—when the host does, and not before.

Gents would also do well to keep in mind that while chivalry isn't what it used to be, it hasn't disappeared either. Haygood teaches her male students to pull chairs out for their dates, and to stand when women leave or return to the table.

"But I don't want to say that it's mandatory," she says, "only because so few young men are even taught to do it these days." Still, it's a nice touch, especially in more traditional crowds.

Finally, when it comes time to leave, resist the urge to duck out surreptitiously (sometimes known, for reasons that for the sake of good manners need not be dredged up, as the Irish goodbye). Whether you're twelve or ninety-two, you simply cannot leave any function—be it a bonfire, a tailgate party, or a formal dinner—without a farewell and thank-you to the person responsible for organizing it. It sounds simple, Haygood says, but people forget to do it all the time.

WEAR A SQUARE

DATING AT LEAST AS far back as ancient Greece, the utilitarian handkerchief saw many a fashion incarnation before it became the pocket square, a sartorial staple of the old-school Southern dress code, before casual Fridays and sportswear became the norm. But through the centuries, this little patch of fabric has retained its practical purpose—to mop a sweaty brow, dry tears, or combat a runny nose—and it looks pretty darn sharp too.

Although there are several standard ways to wear a pocket square, Richmond, Virginia, native Peyton Jenkins, cofounder of the bespoke menswear company Alton Lane, favors the traditional flat fold over fussier peaked versions. "Classic always wins," Jenkins says. "You can't go wrong with the flat fold. It works with a tuxedo, a business suit, or a blazer on the weekend."

Luckily, it also involves just two simple steps: Fold the square in half from left to right, and then nearly in half again from bottom to top, depending on the depth of your pocket. Choose a nice cotton fabric, solid or patterned. "It has more body and is easier to work with than silk," Jenkins says. For a more formal look, wear the pocket square with the smooth folded edge up. Sans tie, flip it 180 degrees and expose the layered edge. Depending on your preference, an eighth to a fourth of an inch of fabric should peek above the pocket.

And no matter how much you might like your handkerchief—or how long you may have spent getting it just so—if a lady needs it, it's hers.

FINGER SALUTES

BY DONOVAN WEBSTER

WE'RE NOT TALKING about rude be-havior here. The opposite, in fact. But this is something that usually happens only on rural Southern two-lanes.

You can't do it on an interstate—or along a six-lane strip of discount malls and big-box stores. And despite what the driving instructors have taught my children—hands at three and nine o'clock to avoid your thumbs' being injured in an air bag deployment—back on the rural roads, I always keep my right hand at twelve o'clock on the steering wheel. That way, when I pass someone going the other way, even a stranger, I can lift my index finger, just to say, "Hi."

It's a thing peculiar to the South. They don't do this in New England or California or Indianapolis. Even in the less urban parts. I know.

The salute can go bigger. If you maybe recognize an acquaintance's car coming from the other direction, you can raise your index *and* middle finger in a kind of double-salute "peace" sign. If it's a friend, you of course switch hands on the wheel and give the whole full-hand wave. If you don't, they're likely to worry you're mad at them. They *know* you saw them.

It's a politeness thing. You know: "I want to acknowledge you." Unless you're in Atlanta, or maybe Charlotte or D.C., nobody honks their horn a heck of a lot. The salute is an antidote to such disturb-ings of the peace.

By now, the salute has gone deep in my

blood. More than once, driving to my farm, I've even given the "Hi" sign to my neighbor's guinea hens, who have a gift for getting out of their pen and out on the road to pick up tiny bits of gravel to help their gullets.

I don't know where it came from. Maybe it's been around since long before Henry Ford got busy, more than a century ago. Maybe we've been hailing each other from carriages, penny-farthing bicycles, horseback, wagons. And I don't know if it'll ever evolve into anything else. But it's there. And the other person usually responds in kind.

I appreciate it.

PUTTING PEN TO PAPER

HONEST-TO-GOD handwritten correspondence may be falling by the wayside these days, but it isn't dead yet. Especially in the South. We're not talking about the standards—birthday cards, holiday greetings, wedding invitations. Just the good old-fashioned letter, whether it's to the neighbor who baked you a pie or to a dear friend for no particular reason at all. It's more than simply being polite. "Handwritten letters are a way for people to deepen relationships," says Elizabeth Edwards, creative director of Charlotte, North Carolina's Arzberger Stationers, one of the oldest such printers in the South. "And it's more important now than ever."

The fact that you simply took the time to put pen to paper is in itself a powerful thing. It's more enduring than a phone call—and certainly above an e-mail, a status update, or any other bit of speedy electronic dispatch. But if you're going to go through the effort, you might as well give it a little flair. Edwards's detail-driven suggestions will take care of the presentation. The message, of course, is up to you.

1. CONSIDER THE PAPER: "Using custom stationery is a way to honor the recipient of your letter, communicating the importance of what you've said, and leaving them with a worthy keepsake. But multicolored designs and patterns can detract from your message, which is why I always encourage my clients to choose something clean and timeless. I recommend soft white or ecru paper for personal stationery. Bright white is typically thought of for commercial use."

2. EMBELLISH SPARINGLY: "There are several easy ways to get creative without interfering with the elegance of the stationery. The first is a tasteful, timeless motif or monogram. A colorful liner is another great way to express yourself. Interesting old-world typefaces can also mix things up."

3. SEAL WITH CARE: "This is something that not many people know: If your envelope has a liner, only wet the tip of the flap. If you wet the entire flap along the edges, the recipient will have to use a letter opener and will destroy the liner in the process."

4. ADDRESS HONESTLY: "Your own handwriting is best. If your penmanship is great, wonderful. If it's not, that's okay, too."

HOW TO TELL A GREAT STORY

BY ROY BLOUNT, JR.

ONE: HAVE AN ANIMAL in your story (or animal products). Two: Show that you are Southern, so people will know what you are doing. I neglected to do this once in an Ohio airport, on my way to see a man who claimed his rooster was able to predict the weather, which turned out to be only partially true. In cases of heavily overcast skies, the rooster would run up under something, and the man, whose name was Adair Treat, would say, "See there? Ten to one we get rain." The rooster's name was Roscoe. He just had a phobia about getting wet. I told Adair Treat, "I have come all this way, and this is all your rooster can do?"

"He can count," Treat said. "Hold up some fingers, any number, I won't look.

Roscoe, see this gentleman here? How many fingers?"

Roscoe didn't let on that he even knew he was being spoken to.

"Well, he's sulled up now. When he senses the presence of somebody lacking confidence in him, he gets into a mind-set of 'I got nothing to prove.'"

But before all that with the rooster, I was talking to these Ohioans in the airport, and I told them about the time I was traveling with a flying squirrel. He had kept chewing his way into our house and gliding from one piece of furniture to the next, and if you've never had that going on in your home periodically, you don't know how upsetting it is. We would capture him, with difficulty, and take him way off up the road, and back he would come. So I was going to fly him to Memphis, where I had business—but while we were going through airport security, he slipped out of his carrier and bounded from one passenger's head to another and on out of sight.

"Oh," said one of the Ohioans, "that's terrible. Can we help you find him?"

"We have a *cat*," another one said, "but we've never flown with her. Are you sure it's wise?"

And I realized I hadn't switched into my Southern accent. As soon as I did, the Ohioans said, "Oh! You're telling a story! That's what you *do*, isn't it? But don't you wear a hat?"

I put on a gimme cap, and after that they interrupted only once more, to ask whether this story was a funny one. So I switched to the straw hat, with the bite out of it.

PARTY LIKE A CAJUN

FROM NEW ORLEANS to Acadiana, February through June marks the season of a deep-rooted Louisiana tradition—the crawfish boil. This is the time to fire up the propane tank, spread the newspapers thick, and get ready to have some fun. It's a laid-back affair. But make no mistake: Folks in Louisiana take their crawfish seriously. Muck it up, and the party might be over faster than you can say "Zatarain's." So do it right.

THE RUB: There are two schools of thought on the proper way to season your mudbugs. A New Orleans–style approach involves boiling the shellfish in water heavily seasoned with cayenne, Tabasco, garlic, lemons, bay leaves, lots of salt, and bags of seafood-boil mix (Zatarain's or Louisiana Crawfish Co., please) for about fifteen minutes. But in Cajun country, the preferred method is to flash-boil the critters for three to five minutes before they're transferred to an ice-filled cooler, crop-dusted with a powdered form of the same spice blend, and left to steam for another forty-five minutes. "That way, that prize piece of yellow fat in the head remains intact," says New Orleans chef Donald Link, a Louisiana native who hits a dozen or more boils each season.

THE BOIL: Remember that the crawfish is the star here. Other than a couple of onions and maybe some halved ears of corn, it doesn't belong in the pot if it wasn't alive when you threw it in there. And even if you're not from Louisiana, your crawfish probably should be. Look for a proven, well-reviewed mail-order outfit, and aim to have the sacks arrive a day early so you can pick out any that didn't survive the trip and clean the mud off of the rest by submerging them in water for three to four hours before cooking. Figure three pounds per person, "or five to seven if the crowd's experienced," Link says. Store your sacks in a cool, shady spot (60 degrees max) until it's time to boil.

THE BREW: Since half the day is spent cooking and socializing and the other half eating, beer is arguably the second-most important thing on the menu. Stock up on something that's light but has a good hoppy kick, to cut through all the spices. "I like Bayou Teche's LA-31," Link says, "but really, Budweiser, Miller Lite, anything easy-drinking will do."

NICE HAT, PARDNER

IN 1866, JUST AFTER the Civil War, Will Harris's great-grandfather settled the Bluffton, Georgia, ranch known today as White Oak Pastures. More than a century later, Harris made waves by converting the ranch from a standard industrialized cattle operation into a model of free-range sustainability. But the gravel-voiced cattleman is hardly your stereotypical crunchy organic farmer. "I'm a cowboy," he says. "And I always say that a well-dressed cowboy doesn't have to know but four things: Stetson, Carhartt, Wrangler, and Justin."

Harris's hat of choice is the Stetson Open Road, a simple, short-brimmed hat that also graced the heads of his father and grandfather. (Our thirty-sixth president, Lyndon Baines Johnson, wore the versatile lid, too—so often, in fact, that it is still referred to in some circles as an "LBJ hat.") Somewhere between a full-on cowboy hat and a fedora, with a deep cattleman's crease that highlights its agricultural pedigree, the Open Road pays respect to an understated Southern cowboy culture that predates that of the American West.

"Growing up, all we watched on TV were westerns," Harris says. "If you really look into the history, though, you'll find that so many of those western cowboys came from the South. I mean, this region was settled by herdsmen. The cowboy culture here runs deep, but it's cowboy culture with a Baptist influence."

Harris and his predecessors have

forgone fancy saddles—influenced, like the wide-brimmed cowboy hats popular out west, by a more flamboyant Mexican cowboy culture—in favor of pared-down seats without much ornamentation. Flashy belt buckles? Not for these cowboys. "My belt is a big, wide brown belt without any fancy buckle," he says. And his shoes are the hardy, reinforced lace-ups known as packer boots.

A man of many innovative ideas about ranching, Harris has sartorial tastes that remain decidedly simple. "I don't own a shirt that isn't Carhartt, a pair of pants that aren't Wrangler blue jeans, or a pair of shoes that aren't Justin boots," he says. "When I go to the beach—well, I don't really go to the beach. My legs will blind your ass. You need a welding mask to look at them in the sun."

A FEW WORDS ABOUT SEERSUCKER

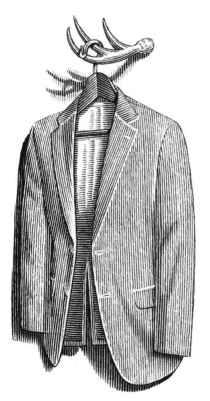

CONSENSUS HOLDS THAT a New Orleans tailor named Joseph Haspel probably cut the first Southern seersucker suit in the first decade of the twentieth century. The light, puckered fabric took off in the South for the same reason that it did in its native India: It's made to handle tropical-strength heat and humidity.

But while we can all agree that seersucker feels good at the height of July, a full set of rumpled stripes isn't always the way to go. "I only wear a full seersucker suit two or three times a year, depending on how many weddings are going on," says acclaimed Florence, Alabama–based designer Billy Reid, who has brought Southern-inspired fashion to the world stage. "When I do seersucker, I usually just wear the jacket. And I tend to keep it more casual."

A seersucker jacket, Reid says, works for anything from a nice dinner to a day at the beach, where a man can even dress it down with shorts. Reid typically pairs his with long pants in muted shades like khaki or light gray. "Keep it simple," he says. Whether in a seersucker jacket or a full suit, forgo the iconic white buck for darker-colored leather shoes or boots. And leave your collar open (no tie) for a little extra breathing room during the dog days of summer.

But the most important rule to wearing seersucker, Reid says, is also one of the oldest: Stay in season. "I don't believe in too many fashion rules. I tend to think they can be pushed. But with seersucker, you should keep it from about April to August."

GET INVITED BACK

RAUCOUS COCKTAIL parties, intimate dinners, weekend guests—Southerners tend to enjoy opening up their homes. Our famous hospitality is built on a foundation of good manners and reciprocity, though, which makes the Southern host acutely appreciative of a gracious houseguest—and equally disdainful of those who fall short. You don't need an etiquette lesson to follow the well-worn principles of common courtesy: Just remember the Golden Rule. But try these tips to go beyond the basics—like making the bed—and really impress your host.

1. BEAR A MEMORABLE GIFT: Sure, some good wine or a bottle of bourbon is nice, but set yourself apart with a more personal gift—a beautifully bound edition of a favorite book, for instance, or customized letterpress stationery. Also key: choosing a gift your hosts will use and enjoy after you're gone, not one they might feel pressure to serve during your visit. Try a planter filled with a ready-made herb garden or some mosquito-repellent citronella for the porch.

2. PITCH IN: Everyone will give a cursory "Can I help?" Few folks actually put some thought into it. Be specific: Offer to walk the dog or set the table. Just finished dinner? "Let me do the dishes." But if your offer to assist is declined, get out of the way. Badgering to help can be as exasperating as expecting to be waited on.

3. GO WITH THE FLOW: Pay attention to how your hosts run the household and follow along with a smile. It's their home, so honor their rules—even if that means leaving your shoes at the door. So, too, their schedule. If everyone else is up and rolling by 8:00 a.m., it's probably not such a great idea to come stumbling out bleary-eyed and pajama-clad at noon.

4. GIVE SOME SPACE: Don't expect to be entertained and fed constantly during your stay. Independence is a virtue among houseguests. Pack books and magazines, go for a walk, or plan a couple of quick side trips to give your hosts a few hours to relax and unwind.

5. SAY THANKS: The power of a handwritten thank-you note can't be overstated. Just be prompt about it. A good Southern host will most likely follow up with his or her own note thanking you for the visit, and you'll want yours to arrive first.

THE SOUTHERN WOMAN'S CLOSET

"ONE OF THE MANY wonderful things about Southern women is that they're always dressed for the occasion," says award-winning clothing designer and Texas native Lela Rose. "Sweatpants are never an option." Janie Bryant, a Tennessee native and costume designer for the television series *Mad Men*, echoes that sentiment and credits her grandmother with instilling in her early on that attention to the little things can make a big impact when it comes to style. You don't need a closet bursting with runway-ready pieces to look put together. Their timeless recommendations add polish without a lot of primping.

1. AN HERMÈS SCARF: Rooted in equestrian tradition, each Hermès silk scarf is a wearable piece of art. "The history of an Hermès scarf is as rich as the vibrant colors woven into these classic pieces," Bryant says. Knot under the chin, belt at the waist, tie to a handbag, or tame flyaway hair—its enduring style will make it a wardrobe mainstay for decades.

2. A CRISP TRENCH COAT: Although the trench coat originated as part of British airmen's uniforms during the First World War, a modern ladies' version offers chic protection against the elements that can be worn over work wear or evening dress. "I've been wearing the same trench coat for nearly ten years,"

Rose says. "It goes with everything and is beautifully timeless."

3. A JUDITH LEIBER MINAUDIÈRE: After receiving a shipment of metal evening bags, known as minaudières, from Italy that arrived dented, Leiber camouflaged the imperfections with Austrian crystals, launching a line of bejeweled clutches that are worthy of being handed down for generations. "They're made in a candy-aisle variety of shapes," Bryant says. "But her custom monogram minaudières act like modern-day family crests. They're truly iconic, signature pieces."

4. A "STATEMENT" NECKLACE: A strand of pearls has its own iconic place in the Southern jewel box, but a bold, colorful necklace is an easy way to add everyday flash and fun. "For the laziest fashion days, it can spruce up any outfit," Rose says.

5. COWBOY BOOTS: Invest in a well-made pair, and with a little care, they only get better with age. "I've loved my pair through and through," Rose says. "And they adjust shockingly well to city life."

THE SOUTHERN MAN'S CLOSET

PAUL TRIBLE WAS working and living in London when he fell in love with good tailoring. The shops of Savile Row taught him the difference between one size fits all and clothes made to fit well and last. But when Trible launched Ledbury, the upscale clothing line that he developed with fellow expat—and Oxford graduate student—Paul Watson, he did so in his native Virginia. Today, the company combines English tailoring with Southern sensibilities in a former tobacco warehouse in downtown Richmond. "There is a great sense of personal style in the South," Trible says. "It's not flashy, but it is classic and often passed down through the generations." Trends come and go, but Trible recommends well-made versions of these five essentials to keep a man looking good for a lifetime.

1. GINGHAM SHIRTS: "In the South, men love patterns—mostly because Southern women love patterns, and, when it comes down to it, that's what's important," Trible says. Gingham shirts in blue, purple, and even pink let a man show some personality without being over-the-top.

2. A LINEN SPORT COAT: The sport coat may be the most versatile item in a man's closet, but it pays to have one you can throw on comfortably in summer. "Most men in the South know a little bit about fabric, simply because it's hot down here,

and the differences between wool and linen become increasingly clear the closer you get to August."

3. A POCKET SQUARE: Trible advises sticking to white or subtle patterns. "A simple cotton pocket square can transform a typical office uniform into evening attire."

4. AN EQUESTRIAN BELT: "Things that are made simply tend to last. A belt made from English bridle leather is a purchase that you will only need to make once." A hoof-pick buckle adds a nice bit of style to a piece of clothing better known for function than form.

5. PADDOCK BOOTS: In dark brown or black leather, these ankle-high boots pair well with most anything from a T-shirt and jeans to a nice suit. "They are more country lawyer than cowboy."

RAISE A GLASS WITH CONFIDENCE

SOUTHERN ORATORY IS not the sole province of elaborately whiskered statesmen of the musty past, though there are certainly sterling and oft-quoted exemplars. It's a tradition that carries through to the present day, and most everybody at one time or another will face a particularly fraught moment of public dis course: the wedding toast, which can cause even the most experienced speaker to go off the rails.

Etiquette expert Diane Gottsman, of the Protocol School of Texas, can tell you stories to curdle your champagne. "Roasting instead of toasting happens way too often," she says. "People like to hear themselves talk, and when they make jokes at the expense of the bride or groom or whomever, it only fuels the fire if people laugh, even nervously. You need someone with a hook to take a bad toaster offstage." If you'd rather not suffer a vaudevillian extraction from the spotlight, follow Gottsman's advice for giving a worthy, and classy, send-off.

First and foremost, be prepared. "A beautiful toast has everything to do with planning and rehearsing—but still making it seem off the cuff," Gottsman says. Still, that doesn't mean there isn't a little room to go with the flow, so don't get flustered if your perfectly planned speech doesn't go quite so perfectly. "When you stand up, it's okay if it doesn't come out exactly how it was planned. Roll with whatever you feel. Have confidence."

Just remember this really isn't about you, so keep the focus off of yourself and on the honorees. "You may be a small part of the story," Gottsman says, "but you should not be the story." And whatever you do, "absolutely no anecdotes about people's exes."

Finally, if you think you might be going on too long, you probably are. "My philosophy is keep it short and sweet: Stand up, speak up, and then shut up," Gottsman says. "There are people waiting behind you." If you're having trouble figuring out how to close in style, don't overthink it. "Remember that everyone loves the sound of their own name: 'We all wish you love, happiness, and long life,' and then name the bride and groom. And certainly get their names right and pronounce them correctly. Which can be difficult if you've had too much to drink."

ROCK A PAIR OF WHITE BUCKS

SOUTHERNERS HAVE been suckers for the white buck ever since the shoe's Jazz Age inception. It most likely has something to do with the warm weather, or maybe it's just that Southerners have never been particularly shy about making a statement. But though the heat endures, the snowy suede on our streets these days has dwindled. There's no reason to fear the white buck. It's still a way to proclaim your Southern gentlemanliness, as long as you follow a few simple guidelines, courtesy of Atlanta tastemaker and menswear designer Sid Mashburn.

1. KEEP IT SEASONAL: Although some folks consider it acceptable to wear white bucks as early as Easter, Mashburn prefers sticking to summer. "I won't put them on before Memorial Day, and never after Labor Day," he says.

2. COORDINATE YOUR OUTFIT: "White bucks go with shorts, jeans, a suit. Denim, khaki, gray wool. I prefer them without socks. But if you do wear socks, they need to be a cream color." Most important, "there must be an edge to the outfit: rolled sleeves, some dirt on the bucks. Something that makes you look less precious."

3. NEVER PULL A FULL CLEVELAND: What the heck is a full Cleveland, you ask? "A full Cleveland is a leisure-suit-era leftover, when you wear a white belt

to match your shoes. Go with something woven, a needlepoint or ribbon belt, instead."

4. KEEP THE FAITH: Mashburn knows white bucks aren't as easy-wearing as, say, loafers or boat shoes, but he says their otherness is precisely the point. "White bucks are misunderstood. You know, you could walk into some places and guys might fight you for wearing them. But you need to be ready to fight. Take a blow for the white bucks. You know that song 'Be Young, Be Foolish, Be Happy'? That's a white-bucks song. A guy who wears white bucks is ready to party."

A HAT FOR THE DERBY

THOUGHT TO BRING the wearers good luck on race day, Kentucky Derby hats are nearly as talked about as the horses themselves—maybe more. The stylish custom is credited to the race's founding father, Colonel M. Lewis Clark, Jr. (grandson of Lewis and Clark explorer William Clark, by the way), who envisioned the event in the grand tradition of European horse racing, where donning festive toppers for ladies was standard practice. And though fashions have changed since the first running of the Derby in the late nineteenth century, Derby hats are as big and bold as ever. So if you are headed to Churchill Downs to drink and laugh and promenade (and watch some horses, too) but aren't sure what to wear, take some advice from designer Christine A. Moore. "Buy the hat first," she says. "You can always find a dress—or five—to match."

The milliner of choice for Kentucky Derby veterans, Moore has more than twenty years of experience in the trade. And whether you're racing royalty or a first-time out-of-towner, navigating styles—from pillboxes to cloches to wide-brim picture hats—is a tricky task. But a few guidelines should abate anxiety and keep you looking smart.

Tackling tradition at the starting gate, Moore advises: "Bigger is not always better. The number-one thing is to go with your personality. The hat should be a reflection of you." If you were hoping to repurpose your favorite old straw beach hat, though, think again. "You should look elegant—feminine and elegant. That's part of the whole allure."

For a flattering fit, "you want the crown of your hat to appear wider than your cheekbones," Moore says, "and always make sure there's air between the brim and your shoulders—even if you choose an oversize brim. You don't want to look like you're wearing an umbrella." But no matter the topper, Moore recommends that you situate it at a slight angle. "It's a look that's universally pleasing." Although if you have an oval face, she says, you can wear a hat straight on with equal style.

Moore suggests the small, chic caps known as fascinators for no-fail sophistication. A European look, they work on just about everyone. The trim should hit at your hair's natural part, to draw the eye in. Bonus: no hat hair, since this style is usually designed around a band or clip.

For styles where mussed hair *is* an issue, borrow a trick from our friends across the Atlantic: "Put pin curls in the very top layer of your hair before putting your hat on," Moore says. "After the race, remove the curls for fresh hair."

What about the guys? "More and more men are wearing hats now," Moore says. "Try a simple fedora or trilby." Keep it classic. Like putting it all on the long shot to win.

THE ART OF GOODBYE

BY DONOVAN WEBSTER

MY WIFE AND her two sisters are nice girls from Memphis. They're also all a lot of fun, not to mention all being pretty great cooks. But when entertaining, as much fun as they are, they know where to draw the line. And yet they do it in a gentle and stately way. They know how to get guests out of the house with a subtleness that . . . hasn't always been my hallmark.

Once, when I was in college, a nice girl from Louisville was visiting my house—for reasons to remain undisclosed—and criticizing everything in it. (But, come to think of it, the place was pretty stark.) Finally, when I couldn't take her negative energy anymore, I pointed.

"Well," I said, "there's the door."

My wife and her family, on the other hand, never miss. They invite guests, feed and water and drink and dessert them, and then, just before the evening begins to lose steam, switch gears and become ramrods wrapped in velvet. Their mother taught them well.

My wife may have the ultimate move. Often, while still sitting at the table—or up in the kitchen after supper, having coffee or another drink as we're doing dishes—she changes modes. She wants her life to be private again. I know her well enough that I can see the change come across her face. She looks up from the table or turns from the sink and smiles—her blue eyes harder—and says, "Well, this *has* been fun . . ."

Any guests who don't get it are allowed a few more minutes—maybe ten—before Janet says, "Hey, let me help you . . . Do you have coats? Let me get your coats."

By now, even the most boorish (or beerish) of guests understands it's time to go. Then she leads them toward the door.

I've learned from the three Chisholm girls and no longer point toward the door. Usually, I offer to walk the guests down our dark drive toward their cars as my wife stands on the porch and waves in the light of the lamps. "Come on *baaack*," she always says. And you can't tell if she means it or not.

★

Part Three

DRINK

DRINK LIKE A SOUTHERNER

BY JONATHAN MILES

WHETHER SOUTHERNERS DRINK MORE THAN THEIR REGIONAL BRETHREN—MORE OFTEN, THAT IS, OR MORE IMMODERATELY, OR, AS IN NEW ORLEANS AND SEC COLLEGE TOWNS, BOTH—CAN BE DEBATED ELSEWHERE. MY ARGUMENT TODAY, PROFFERED WITH THE WARBLY CERTITUDE ONE DERIVES FROM A SECOND GLASS OF BOURBON, IS THAT SOUTHERNERS DRINK BETTER THAN AMERICANS ELSEWHERE. (QUANTITY, AFTER ALL, IS NOT QUALITY, THOUGH AT A CERTAIN TIPPING POINT IN THE EVENING THEY CAN SOMETIMES SEEM TO RUN OFF INTO THE WOODS TOGETHER.)

I should preface this, however, with some clarifications: I do not mean to suggest that what Southerners drink is liquidly superior to what is drunk elsewhere, though often it is. From the South came bourbon, came Antoine Peychaud's invention of the Sazerac, the first codified American cocktail; from the North, Long Island Iced Tea. Yet my poor throat still bears scar tissue from the moonshine sold at a now-defunct juke joint in Holly Springs, Mississippi, which not even an eight-to-one ratio of Mello Yello could mellow, and which was otherwise useful because it not only removed paint but the metal beneath it. And while the South possesses its share of beer snobs, they are marginal figures, like trout anglers; the primary test of a beer in the South is its temperature. No, where Southerners differ—and where they excel—is in *how* they drink: zealously, ebulliently, loquaciously, impiously.

One could lay reasonable credit to the environment, I suppose: When it's 98 degrees outside, a drink is not merely a drink; it's the sensate equivalent of a winning lottery ticket. Or to the theological briars that pricked Southern drinking culture: In a region dominated by Baptists, drinking carried, at best, the tinge of scandal and, at worst, the risk of eternal damnation. Gusto was required to overcome that hard-shell resistance; every drink mattered because, well, that drink might actually matter. To drink like a Southerner one must drink with relish, rather than drab connoisseurship; with a sense of semi-forbidden delight, as when breaking curfew for the first time;

with garrulous abandon, unlike those pinched-faced drinkers one sees in, say, New England taverns, self-medicating beneath the glow of a soundless television; and with a keen appreciation for what Walker Percy, that paragon of the Southern drinker, called the "cumulative bliss" of a glass of bourbon. There are variations to this, of course.

A story I've heard, possibly apocryphal, has it that our great Civil War historian and man of letters Shelby Foote and a certain William Faulkner once made a pilgrimage together to the battlefields of Shiloh, in Tennessee. It was a Sunday morning, but along the way they were able to score some moonshine from a fellow they spotted having his shoes shined, Faulkner's logic being that any man having his shoes shined was likely to know where to find some whiskey. By the time they'd reached the battlefield's famed Peach Orchard, they were loose enough to want to re-enact the great cavalry charge on their own, sabers drawn in their minds.

That's how to drink like a Southerner.

NEW ORLEANS CLASSICS

IN 1795, Antoine Amédée Peychaud fled the strife of his native Saint-Domingue—now Haiti—and shipped out to New Orleans, where the Creole apothecary went on to invent Peychaud's bitters and the now iconic Sazerac. That N'Awlins was already well established as a wild, cultural-gumbo party town is certain, but Peychaud was a pivotal figure in its evolution. Folks had long been mixing alcohol with other stuff, but it's no stretch to say that the Crescent City's rich cocktailing history began with old Antoine.

A couple of hundred Fat Tuesdays after Mr. Peychaud's immigration, New Orleans remains the undisputed cocktail capital of the South. Never mind those gaudy Kool-Aid-red Hurricanes, across the city, bartenders, mixologists, artisanal anesthetists, or whatever you want to call the modern-day practitioners of the Peychaudian arts are keeping tradition alive with some truly great drinks. And while there's nothing better than sipping one in the place where it began, if you want a taste of the Big Easy in your living room, belly up to your home bar and mix some history.

THE COCKTAIL: SAZERAC

MOST MODERN BARKEEPS worth their shakers consider this aromatic cocktail the classic of classics, a straightforward whiskey drink flavored with a hint of bitters, a little sugar, and a swirl of absinthe. Though nowadays a Saz is usually made with rye whiskey, Kirk Estopinal, of Cure, honors the drink's past. Its name comes from the original prime ingredient, Sazerac de Forge et Fils brand cognac, so Estopinal mixes up a smooth, brandy-based variation that features Pierre Ferrand 1840 cognac, a vintage blended to mimic the flavors of early-nineteenth-century New Orleans.

2 oz. Pierre Ferrand 1840 **cognac**
¼ oz. **demerara-sugar syrup**
    (2:1 sugar-to-water ratio)
2 dashes Peychaud's **bitters**
2 dashes **absinthe** (or an anise-flavored
    substitute like Herbsaint or Pernod)
Twist of **lemon**

In a glass or a Boston shaker, combine cognac, demerara syrup, and bitters over ice and stir for roughly 30 seconds with a long-handled bar spoon. In a prechilled rocks glass, pour in the absinthe and swirl to coat the interior, pouring out any excess. Strain the cocktail into the glass, squeeze the lemon twist over the drink, rub the peel side along the rim, then discard the twist or plop it in the glass.

THE COCKTAIL: RAMOS GIN FIZZ

IN A CITY known for its late nights and lost weekends, it's only appropriate that New Orleans should have a group of cocktails tailored for the inevitable rough mornings-after. The historic Ramos Gin Fizz is a great example of this genre: a creamy, approachable brunchtime cocktail with enough gin to take the edge off and the velvety mouthfeel of God's own Dreamsicle. At Arnaud's French 75, bartender and scholar Chris Hannah gives his traditional version its ethereal lightness with a few solid minutes of hard shaking. It's the only way to get it right.

1½ oz. **gin**

1 oz. **simple syrup** (1:1 sugar-to-water ratio)

½ oz. fresh-squeezed **lemon juice**

½ oz. fresh-squeezed **lime juice**

1 **egg white** (pasteurized)

1 oz. **heavy cream**

3 drops **orange flower water**

1 oz. **club soda**, chilled

In a shaker, combine all ingredients except soda and shake vigorously to combine. Add ice cubes and shake again for at least 2 minutes to provide the drink's distinctive silky texture. Strain into a tapered highball glass or wine flute, top with club soda, and stir.

THE COCKTAIL: PIMM'S CUP

THE BAR: BAR TONIQUE

THIS REFRESHING HIGHBALL can claim a dual lineage—a distinctly British drink with a historic New Orleans address.

Made with a spicy English gin–based liqueur (Pimm's No. 1) and a tall pour of lemony soda or ginger ale, this summer quencher is associated with the legendary Napoleon House bar, on Chartres Street. At Bar Tonique, a funky craft-cocktail joint at the edge of the French Quarter, bartenders forgo the traditional cucumber garnish and muddle citrus fruits to order. The result: a distinctively tangy take on the classic.

¼ oz. **demerara-sugar syrup** (2:1 sugar-to-water ratio)

⅓ **lemon** (cut into wedges)

⅓ **lime** (cut into wedges)

⅙ **orange** (cut into wedges)

2 oz. **Pimm's No. 1**

Club soda

In a metal shaker, combine demerara syrup and citrus wedges and crush with a wooden muddler. Add Pimm's and a couple of ice cubes and shake well. Strain into an ice-filled highball glass, fill to the rim with club soda, and stir.

AUTHENTIC DIXIE LEMONADE

EXTRAORDINARILY important in a region that long looked askance at publicly drinking alcohol—especially if a lady was holding the glass—homemade lemonade has been a Southern favorite since even before iced tea ruled the porch. But chances are high that the last swig most folks had of something purporting to be lemonade contained mysterious ingredients like FD&C Yellow No. 5.

Authentic Dixie lemonade is a thing of simplicity and proportion. When you drink it, you know it, because it outshines all the other concoctions and chemistry experiments masquerading as the genuine article. Many of the earliest Southern cookbooks included recipes for lemonade, and the preparation hasn't changed too much since 1824's *The Virginia Housewife*, in which Mary Randolph simply advised mixing freshly pressed lemon juice with water and sugar to taste. Still, that's not much of a recipe. Luckily, we've got a fail-safe method for making the good stuff.

The key is a basic balance and smooth texture, and simple syrup made with regular ol' granulated white cane sugar is the best way to get there. Using a one-to-one ratio, simmer your sugar and water in a saucepan over low heat until the sugar's dissolved and the syrup's clear. Make sure the mixture doesn't boil. Allow the syrup to cool, and keep it refrigerated. Now that you've got a perfectly simple syrup, juice a dozen very fresh, springy-feeling lemons—big organic ones are best—removing the seeds but keeping the pulp for texture and little bursts of flavor. Mix in seven cups of filtered water and three cups of your syrup. You'll find this most refreshing of libations surely worthy of a nineteenth-century Virginia housewife's approval, but should anyone else find it a tad tame, it goes dangerously well with dark Caribbean rum—to taste, of course.

SOUTHERN CITRUS

It wouldn't be summer in the South without fresh-squeezed lemonade. But Southern citrus goes well beyond pucker-inducing yellow fruit. These three varieties are a sweet (and sour) taste of Dixie.

KEY LIME: The thin-skinned little fruit that makes one of the South's favorite pies is smaller and tarter than the Persian lime, its more common cousin. Citrus growers brought it to the Florida Keys in the nineteenth century, and though a 1926 hurricane all but wiped out commercial production, the key lime is still a staple in backyards and front-porch planters.

KUMQUAT: At the height of the Southern winter, ripe kumquats provide much-needed bursts of bright orange color and tongue-tingling flavor. To eat a kumquat, simply roll it between your fingers a few times, which releases the essential oils in the skin, and pop it directly into your mouth—no peeling required. Just be mindful of the seeds.

RUBY RED GRAPEFRUIT: The grapefruit is a New World hybrid that evolved in Barbados sometime in the eighteenth century and later migrated to Texas with waves of settlers and missionaries. There, it took root in the warm Rio Grande Valley, where a mutation on a pink grapefruit tree created the popular Ruby Red.

THE PERFECT BAR—AND WHY THE
SOUTH HAS SO MANY OF THEM

BY GUY MARTIN

TOWARD THE END OF R. L. Burnside's life, some television producers selected the North Mississippi blues shouter's bleak, magisterial ode "Woke Up This Morning" as the opening theme for *The Sopranos*. A little money began lapping at R. L.'s ankles. Not much changed for him except that he had to padlock his refrigerator with a stout porch-swing chain run through the handle—relatives and friends had begun dropping by when he was out and helping themselves to the potables, on the theory that the TV money would automatically refill the icebox.

"I made a New Year's resolution," he announced at a concert during this period. "I decided I was gonna quit drinkin', unless I was by myself or with somebody."

Taking a cue from his impeccable logic, this is our theory: The South has produced such excellent establishments in which to drink "with somebody" because we have created such a cornucopia of fine, local, organically grown reasons to drink. Here are a few: Fishing. No fishing. Summer. Failing summer, Mardi Gras. Weeklong cotillions and/or "telephone book" weddings. Recovery from weeklong cotillions and/or "telephone book" weddings. SEC football championship, won. SEC football championship, lost. Cotton crop, good. Cotton crop, bad.

And so forth, covering every aspect of

life, place, season, and hour of the day. The bars of the South have been designed to cradle and nurture this universe of infinite possibility. Take the dark, beautiful Esquire Tavern in San Antonio, established in 1933. The Esquire fronts onto Commerce Street but backs onto the River Walk—so that the caballeros entering the long, tin-ceilinged room are accompanied on the left for the entire distance from street to river by nearly a hundred feet of oak bar. Walking along it, you think it will stop because the Texas boys must have eventually run out of wood. But—like Texas as a place and Texans as a people—the Esquire's bar doesn't stop until it hits the river. Being in the Esquire is by definition being "at" the bar.

Great Southern bars are often at the edge of something big. At the Lorelei, the Islamorada watering hole on Upper Matecumbe Key, in the Florida Keys—beloved by backcountry guides and fishermen—a snowy egret patrols the rail next to the bar. Nobody pays him any mind, which is why he's so comfortable hopping from the rail to the tables as the guides assess the tides and the moon and the performance of the tarpon over drinks at sunset. The egret is straight out of a Melville novel, a portentous beast of the wilderness, standing sentinel as the fishermen plot yet another invasion of his territory. The Lorelei is the last bit of civilization the guides see as they make the twenty-five-mile run in their skiffs for the backcountry—and the first bit of civilization they see as they return.

And then—at the other end of the socioeconomic spectrum from a bar catering to $600-a-day guides and the anglers who can afford them—there is the juke joint. I once visited the storied R. L. Burnside kitchen and tested the refrigerator chain personally, on an evening when a few of us had driven over to beg him to play a couple of sets at Junior Kimbrough's juke joint, outside Holly Springs, Mississippi. Burnside never locked his door. He just locked the refrigerator. The chain was on, which meant no R. L. We went to Junior's anyway, hoping to find him there. He wasn't. But his hyperkinetic grandson, drummer Cedric Burnside, was, and he played like the devil incarnate.

Junior's has since burned to the ground, as a result of what we might call terminal juke-joint-ness—meaning, the unholy combination of frayed 1930s wiring in a sharecropper's house with moonshine in the larder. Technically, as a bar, Junior's had nothing to recommend it. The moonshine could eat the deposits off a junkyard carburetor, and the beer was worse. But before its inevitable metamorphosis into an ash heap, Junior's did have the rockingest house band in the South: Junior himself on guitar, R. L. on guitar, and Cedric on drums. After Junior died, the Kimbroughs and their associates kept doling out the dollar beers and the 'shine, R. L. and Cedric kept playing when they didn't have paying gigs, and people kept driving in from miles around to dance on the busted linoleum.

In addition to the superb music, there were a couple of other Southern peculiarities. One was that nobody tried too hard. If Junior's family had been trying harder, they might have offered something to eat besides the overcooked hot dogs or found some slightly more palatable forms of swill. They didn't. This bred an unapologetic, you're-in-our-living-room level of hospitality. Anybody could walk into Junior's and dance their ass off—anybody: the working people of Holly Springs, professors from Oxford, fans of R. L.'s from around the region. Junior's effortlessly accomplished that stripped-down thing that often occurs in great Southern bars: It dove for the low end with such force and velocity that it punched through the bottom and came out on top.

And that is the mark of a perfect bar.

RAISE YOUR BAR

FOR SOME SOUTHERNERS, a good bottle of bourbon is about the only bar tool they need. Others elevate the home bar to high art. If you fall somewhere in the middle, a few smart additions beyond the standard bar-tool arsenal—jigger, shaker, strainer, muddler, etc.—can give even a modest home setup a pro touch. And they won't cost you a fortune,

either. Fourth-generation New Orleans bartender Chris McMillian, cofounder of the Museum of the American Cocktail, maintains that the best bar upgrades are the simplest.

1. LEWIS BAG AND MALLET: According to McMillian, "What defines Southern drinking is our temperature and climate, so the ability to manipulate ice is important." One of his favorite tools, this bag allows home bartenders to create perfectly dry crushed ice—just right for making juleps.

2. VINTAGE COCKTAIL SKEWERS: The golden age of mixed drinks and the art deco era just barely overlapped, but the period still produced a stunning array of stylish nibble picks and swizzle

sticks that you can still find at vintage-minded shops. Guests always appreciate "a beautiful accoutrement," McMillian says.

3. SUGARCANE: In addition to making a handsome garnish, sugarcane produces a subtle sweetness that pays tribute to the South's Caribbean influences. Pressed cane juice is ideal for mixing daiquiris.

4. ORANGE BITTERS: Assuming you've already stocked up on Angostura and Peychaud's, McMillian suggests adding a bottle of high-quality orange bitters, a pre-Prohibition staple. A dash of orange bitters brightened up the original martini. Try some in yours for a little turn-of-the-century flavor.

5. FAMOUS NEW ORLEANS DRINKS & HOW TO MIX 'EM, BY STANLEY CLISBY ARTHUR: More than any esoteric liqueur, Southern bartenders need grace, decorum, and a sense of theatricality, McMillian says. When he manned the bar, for example, he was known for extemporaneously reciting an 1892 ode to the mint julep. More than just a recipe tome, Arthur's seminal 1937 book is crammed with inspiration for cocktailing *and* storytelling.

HAVE PUNCH, WILL PARTY

"THE NUMBER OF PUNCHES traditional in Southern society is astronomical," Eugene Walter once marveled. A writer, chef, and inveterate bon vivant, Walter was born in Mobile, Alabama, caught matinees there with Truman Capote as a kid, and later hung out with such luminaries as Fellini, Eliot, and Faulkner. He was also a remarkably talented party host who could extract festivity out of a few loaves of bread, peanut butter, dill pickles, and some bacon. All of his punches were designed for celebration, which is to say they featured plenty of sparkling wine. Walter suggested combining chilled champagne with candied ginger, white rum, and cognac or stirring two bottles of bubbly into a bowlful of red wine, brandy, and sugar. Sounds like a recipe for a party bound to end early or badly or both—or go on and on, outrageously, depending on the guest list.

But one of the most storied (and potent) champagne-enhanced party mixes is the Chatham Artillery Punch, described by Walter as a "famous Savannah charmer." Indeed, it takes only a cup or two for most drinkers to fall under the spell of this tasty tipple, which takes its name from Georgia's oldest military unit and may date back to the colonial era. Early documentation of the drink is sparse, since an imbibing session doesn't put most folks in the mood to journal, but it was almost certainly served in 1819, when President James Monroe stopped by Savannah. Back then, the stuff was mixed up in a horse bucket, but it works just as well when prepared in a silver bowl or a plastic cooler, whether you're partying in honor of an engagement or a game.

The following preparation is from Damon Lee Fowler, author of *The Savannah Cookbook*. Starting at least two days before you plan to serve some Chatham Artillery, soak two ounces of green tea leaves in a quart of cold water. After a day and a half or so, mix the infused water with the juice of three lemons and a half pound of light brown sugar. Add one quart apiece of dark rum, brandy, and bourbon or rye. Let all that mingle at room temperature for at least eight hours before you pour it over a block of ice and add three bottles of champagne.

Then stand back.

SWEET TEA: A LOVE STORY

BY ALLISON GLOCK

MY MOTHER'S SWEET TEA was not the best. Perhaps this is because she was from West Virginia, a place where people drink sweet tea with some ambivalence. Or maybe because in Jacksonville, Florida, where I was raised, delicious sweet tea could be found for $1.99 at the local supermarket in sweaty gallon jugs with nothing but the word *sweet* and the date stamped on the plastic.

She still made sweet tea, of course, being a Southern woman of whom having iced tea on hand is expected. But instead of sugar, my mother used Sweet'N Low, which is kind of like making chocolate cake with dirt. She insisted no one could tell the difference: "They're both *sweet*."

For most of my youth, any sweet tea I consumed came from fast-food restaurants, usually those specializing in fried chicken or ribs. Soda was not allowed in our bodies or even our house—except for Tab, for Mother, until they figured out the chemical that made Tab sweet also made rats insane. Then, all soft drinks were verboten. Sweet tea, however, was fine, even though the health benefits of drinking sweet tea are akin to those of drinking icing.

My father, a doctor, explained to me that sweet tea is the devil's brew, blood-sugar-wise. A glass of sweet tea is around 22 percent sugar, twice that of a can of cola. Add to that the free refills one is accustomed to getting with sweet tea, and you're looking at enough sugar to choke Augustus Gloop.

When you drink sweet tea, your body starts to pump out insulin like water from a fire hose. Then, you have the caffeine. Which stimulates your adrenaline. Which confuses your metabolism. And keeps you from feeling sated, as one normally would after swallowing that much sweetness. Only a select few can eat seven pieces of cheesecake at a sitting, for example. But nearly everyone I know nods and says, "Just one more" when the lunch lady comes around toting the clear pitcher with the rubber band snapped around the handle. Say what you will, but sweet tea is the real hillbilly heroin.

To say Southerners drink sweet tea like water is both true and not. True because the beverage is served at every meal, and all times and venues in between—at church and at strip clubs, at preschool and in nursing homes. Not true because unlike water or wine or even Coca-Cola, sweet tea *means* something. It is a tell, a tradition. Sweet tea isn't a drink, really. It's culture in a glass. Like Guinness in Ireland. Or ouzo in Greece.

(When I was stuck in New York for a stint, a bout of homesickness led me to get the words *sweet tea* tattooed on my left arm. I could think of nothing else that so perfectly encapsulated the South of my pining. Now that I have moved home, it serves less as a touchstone and more as a drink order.)

Theories abound: Southerners prefer sweet tea because back in the day we used sugar as a preservative and our palates grew to crave the taste. Southerners like sweet tea because it is served ice cold and it is hot as biscuits down here. Southerners like sweet tea because we are largely descended from Celts and Brits, making a yearning for tea a genetic imperative. Southerners like sweet tea because Southerners are poor and tea is cheap. (Cheaper than beer anyway.) Southerners like sweet tea because it is nonalcoholic but it still gives you a hearty, if somewhat diabolical, buzz.

No matter the source, our affection for sweet tea characteristically reaches religious fervor. Ask any Southerner where the best sweet tea is served, and he or she will have an opinion. I once knew a man who would drive forty-five minutes to a South Georgia Chick-fil-A because it had what he deemed the tea of the gods. This is not the sort of devotion one finds with other beverages, even coffee. Coffee is an addiction. Sweet tea is an obsession.

We are similarly evangelical about how best to prepare sweet tea. The basic recipe is undemanding. You brew a handful of bags of Lipton or Luzianne or whatever pekoe you prefer, pour the hot tea over a mound of sugar or simple syrup, add water to dilute to taste, stir, and serve over ice, with or without lemon. The amount of sugar is up to the maker, but generally runs somewhere between cotton candy sweet and sweet enough to liquefy your teeth.

Some people like to get fancy. Adding raspberries, using a coffeemaker to brew the blend, sneaking in baking soda to tame the bitterness. These people are annoying. Sweet tea should be just that. Any differences should come from the alchemy of proportion and tea selection, not questionable, post-brewed, kitchen-sink-ian doctoring. Save that for BBQ sauce. (Also irritating: the nouveau

tradition of some restaurants serving the tea unsweet, with a little jug of simple syrup on the side. Sweet tea isn't meant to be precious. It is a guzzle drink.)

Recipes for sweet tea exist from the turn of the nineteenth century on, but lessen in frequency starting around the 1930s. By then, everybody knew how to make sweet tea, and recipes became unnecessary, like instructions for walking.

In 1879 Marion Cabell Tyree published *Housekeeping in Old Virginia*, which many believe contains the first printed sweet tea recipe. Tyree advocates "a squeeze of lemon," writing that lemon "will make this delicious and healthful, as it will correct the astringent tendency."

By the 1920s Americans were stocking their kitchens with specialized iced tea glasses, long spoons, and dainty lemon forks. In *Southern Cooking*, published in 1928, Henrietta Stanley Dull advises women to serve sweet tea with "a sprig of mint, a strawberry, a cherry, a slice of orange, or pineapple." "Milk," she writes, "is not used in iced tea." (No word on Sweet'N Low.)

South Carolina was the first place in the United States to grow commercial tea, an industry founded in the late 1700s when French explorer and botanist André Michaux stopped by with a tea plant in his satchel. He also brought crape myrtles and camellias. If he'd imported a hog, we'd have statues to the guy in every Southern town square. For some time, sweet tea was a sign of wealth. Sugar and ice cost money. To be able to use both in a drink was flashing serious old-timey bling. Then refrigeration happened. And any garden-variety cracker could have tea with ice. Sugar got cheaper, then ubiquitous, and with it, sweet tea.

It is impossible to imagine eating most Southern foods without sweet tea. You can't wash down pulled pork with water. It takes a beverage with some oomph to cut through lard-dunked catfish. The sugar in sweet tea is nature's intestinal Drano. The caffeine makes it possible to drive home after a Sunday brunch of fried chicken and cheese grits. This is not to say sweet tea goes with everything—pizza requires Coke, curry requires beer—only that it marries best with the food of our

people, cementing its status as the iconic Southern libation.

In 2003 Georgia representative John Noel introduced House Bill 819 proposing to require all Georgia restaurants that serve tea to offer sweet tea, defined in the bill as "iced tea which is sweetened with sugar at the time that it is brewed." The bill—which warned that "any person who violates this Code section shall be guilty of a misdemeanor of a high and aggravated nature"—was a joke, but Noel reportedly said he wouldn't mind if it actually passed into law.

My sweet tea addiction came into full bloom not in Georgia, where I lived for many years and enjoyed many a first-rate glass of sweet tea, but in Knoxville, Tennessee, at a modest family-run tearoom called the Chintzy Rose.

The Chintzy Rose is a side-of-the-road junk shop/café that sells painted furniture and chenille throws along with BBQ and corn chowder. Run by Bobbie Miller and her daughter Kelly Phibbs, it offers superior chicken salad and strawberry cake, but what brings in folks from as far away as Utah is the sweet tea.

The tea at the Chintzy Rose transcends the beverage category. It is more of a meal. A song. A poem. Notes of orange and lemon intertwine with the sharpness of the tea, all of it buoyed by a mysterious sweetness unlike your basic simple syrup. They serve it with an orange wedge in chunky crystal glasses, but it hardly matters. They could serve it out of their shoes and people would still line up to drink. It is the Proust of sweet tea. Complicated, elusive, not for the weak of heart. Every mouthful reveals another layer of flavor. The ladies won't divulge how they make the tea so rich and compelling, citing "secret ingredients." I'm pretty sure one of them starts with *c* and ends with *rack*.

According to Kelly, their tea started as a custom blend supplied on the down low by a guy from the local JFG Coffee Company factory. "He never told us what was in it either." After a time, the ladies made their own concoction: "loose tea—it was a lot of trouble." Now all they'll cop to is "a combination of teas. We always make it strong. Most people in the South like it strong and sweet."

Kelly says she gets a lot of folks who

come only for the sweet tea, $1.75, free refills. "I've had a bunch tell us we should open a drive-through window so they won't have to get out of their cars."

"This woman came in a while back for the first time," remembers Kelly. "And every time I walked out there her glass was empty. By about the fifth trip, I said, 'Again?' She said it would be easier if I just brought an IV and hooked her up."

When I lived in Knoxville, I drank Chintzy Rose tea every day. I had my own table in the back, right by the kitchen, and my first glass of tea was generally waiting there for me before my jeans hit the seat. I could never, no matter how many times I swore to myself beforehand that today would be the day, drink just one glass. My resolve melted with the sugar.

I took others to the Chintzy Rose. Veteran tea drinkers who swore that so-and-so's tea was better until they tasted their first Chintzy sip, then looked at me, their eyes glazed, breath short, speechless with wonder and gratitude. I brought Yankees in too. Folks who had never heard of sweet tea, which was a bit unfair really, because after the Rose, none would compare—kind of like seeing the Beatles for your first concert or learning to drive in a Ferrari.

When I left Knoxville (eight pounds heavier, incidentally), I begged Kelly for the recipe. And by begged, I mean I offered either one of my daughters in trade.

I never got the secret. Since then, I've tried to replicate their sweet tea in my own kitchen. I haven't come close. Still, my mother likes it. I tell her it's like hers, only without the carcinogens. She says she doesn't notice the difference.

A SWEET (TEA) RECIPE

IF YOU'VE ALREADY got a favorite family formula, far be it from anyone to tell you it's not perfect. Sweet tea is personal. Heck, some people even like mixing in a little orange juice (we hear it's not half bad). But if you didn't grow up with it or just need a little help, here's a basic—and classic—recipe to try, and then tinker with as you see fit.

Bring three cups of water to a boil and then add six tea bags. (Any tea will do, but a blend of orange pekoe and black tea is especially suitable for sweetening.) Fred Thompson, author of *Iced Tea*, likes to add a pinch of baking soda to the pot, but if tannins don't scare you, press on without it. Continue to boil for one minute before removing from the heat. Steep for ten minutes. Remove the tea bags, lest the tea become too bitter, stir in a half cup of sugar, and pour into a two-quart pitcher. Fill up the rest with cold water and allow the tea to cool before refrigerating. If you're feeling energetic, pour some of the tea into an ice cube tray and freeze, so you won't have to worry about diluting it when you add ice later. Should you wish to make your tea fancier, you might garnish with a sprig of mint, but there's nothing wrong with a simple lemon wheel, same as waitresses across the South cut at the start of every shift.

ABSINTHE RESURRECTED

IN 1912, on the heels of a misguided European controversy, absinthe was made illegal in the United States—a blow, in particular, to port cities like Charleston, South Carolina, and New Orleans, through which the spirit came to the South in the early nineteenth century. (The latter, seeking a replacement with which to make Sazeracs, eventually came up with the anise-flavored Herbsaint.) Nearly a century later, New Orleanian T. A. Breaux came along and almost single-handedly undid the damage. An environmental scientist and spirits enthusiast, Breaux studied pre-ban absinthe and was able to show that concentrations of thujone—the toxic chemical found in grand wormwood that was thought to give "the green fairy" such wild hallucinogenic properties that it was outlawed—were so low as to be practically nonexistent. The authorities took heed and in 2007 approved the first true absinthe for sale in the United States in ninety-five years.

Ban lifted, Breaux drew on his research (and his world-class collection of century-old absinthes) to launch the first in a series of authentic, award-winning spirits based on chemical reverse engineering and excellent taste. Today, he's the country's—and perhaps the world's—foremost expert on the spirit, and his top-shelf Jade Liqueurs absinthes are the proof.

Quality is an important consideration

with any liquor, but it's particularly important with the green stuff: Unlike, say, bourbon, absinthe is not defined by law. A spirit labeled "absinthe" might indeed be an authentic distillation of the proper botanicals—or it could be some grain alcohol with artificial flavors and food coloring. The latter, much more common than you might think, isn't worth your money or your buzz. Check the fine print on even the most illustrious labels.

Once you've got the real deal, though, how best to enjoy it? Some love to sip it straight, but Breaux prefers the French method: Drip three parts ice-cold water into one part absinthe—and slowly, to best bring out the subtle aromatics. This transforms the green spirit into an opalescent milk known as the *louche*. Though some opt to dissolve a sugar cube in the mixture, Breaux prefers his absinthe unsweetened. Contrary to legend, he says, sugar has always been optional, a way to make the cheap stuff more palatable, and only masks the complexity of a quality absinthe.

In the nineteenth-century South, absinthe was enjoyed in the French style, but warm weather quickly gave rise to the cooling absinthe frappé. To make it, shake a shot or two of absinthe with ice and a dash of simple syrup. Strain into an ice-filled glass, top with a couple of ounces of soda water, and garnish with mint. "It's a potent, refreshing drink suited to our Southern climate," Breaux says.

But back in those early days, despite its high alcohol content, absinthe, along with bitters, was considered an herbal medicine, a healing elixir. In the morning, folks would mix them in a tonic with some brandy and a spoonful of sugar ("to make the medicine go down," Breaux says), knock back the concoction, and head to work. Sound familiar? You may have a problem—or you may simply recognize our old friend the Sazerac.

THE ONE AND ONLY MINT JULEP

BY JONATHAN MILES

ASIDE FROM THE MARTINI, the mint julep may be the most iconic cocktail in America. There's not a citizen alive who hasn't heard of it, which is more than you can say for the manhattan, the cosmopolitan, the sidecar, and the Negroni, all of which outsell mint juleps by a staggeringly wide margin. And that, mind you, is if you can even locate the rare bartender willing to fix you one. So here's the saloon riddle for the day: If we know and adore mint juleps—"the very dream of drinks," as a Kentucky newspaperman named J. Soule Smith wrote, accurately, in the 1890s—so damn much, then why don't we drink them? Allow me to cut you off before you tell me about your last Derby Day party: Sorry, that doesn't count. A drink this sublime—"the zenith of man's pleasure," Mr. Smith went on—shouldn't be relegated to sipping just one day a year, like a fruitcake waiting for Christmas. It does not require, as a garnish, a televised horse race and a bunch of Yankees doing

Foghorn Leghorn imitations. Nor will I brook the claim that juleps are hard to make. They're no more difficult than all the mojitos that have been creeping their way north from Miami for the past half decade or so. They're easier, in fact, since they don't require a giant sack of limes. No, our weird resistance to drinking mint juleps—let's cue Mr. Smith one more time, before we call him a cab: "He who has not tasted one has lived in vain"—is owing to something else.

Here's my theory: The mint julep has become too iconic to merely drink. It's like the communion wafer of cocktails. For one, there's all the back-and-forth scuffling among historians and professional "alcohologists" (to crib H. L. Mencken's great term) about the inscrutable origins of the drink and the proper and properly authentic way to mix a julep—do you leave the mint in or remove it? Must the ice be crushed? And was the actual cause of the Civil War, as the author Irvin S. Cobb posited in 1936, an obnoxious Northerner adding nutmeg to a mint julep? Then there are those silver julep cups that tradition dictates using.

They're intimidating. And it feels downright silly drinking out of one of those while you're watching the Braves on TV with your other hand nestled in a bowl of Ruffles. (I have a vast collection of those cups, all of them awarded to me for playing the groomsman role in various Southern weddings. In fact, there's one on my desk as I type this. I keep pens in it.) Owing to all this pomp and kerfuffle, drinking a mint julep, to some folks, can feel too much like an affectation, akin to rechristening the porch the veranda, or yourself the Colonel. That's way too much cultural pressure when you're just trying to cool yourself off on a summer afternoon. Makes you want to reach for a Bud and be done with it.

Don't. The mint julep may be sacred in the South, but so is college football, and that doesn't stop us from enjoying it. It's not a tuxedo, requiring a special occasion. It's a drink, a splendid and simple drink, the ideal analgesic to a tough day at work, and the perfect—yes, perfect—counter to the redlining mercury of a hot Southern day. Its central ingredients—mint, bourbon, sugar—do not suffer from clumsy commingling, nor demand engraved vessels, nor mind if you root for the New York Giants so long as Eli is taking the snap. (They will, however, violently boil over if you add nutmeg.) Citizens, it's high time to reclaim the mint julep from the curators, the purists, the tsk-tsking authenticators and frowning archbishops of Southern culture. Think of it like the blues: It's swell that all these archivists are preserving it, and it's great that a microtonal analysis of Robert Johnson's "Drunken Hearted Man" demonstrates Robert's debt to Lonnie Johnson, but, really, shouldn't we all be dancing?

THE MINT JULEP

½ oz. **superfine sugar**
1 oz. **hot water**
8 **mint leaves,** plus one **mint sprig**
2 oz. **bourbon**

DISSOLVE THE SUGAR in the water in an old-fashioned glass (or julep cup, of course). Add the mint leaves and press them lightly with a spoon—you want to seduce the oil from the mint leaves, not beat it out of them. Add the bourbon, fill the glass with cracked ice, stir, and plant the mint sprig in the ice alongside a short straw.

BITTERS, BARBECUED

THE SPIRITS GIVE a drink its character and the mixers its balance, but the addition of aromatic bitters is what lends many classic cocktails their depth—and what better Southern twist on Peychaud's originals than home-brewed bitters born out of a love for barbecue? Mixologists often make their own bitters by infusing Everclear or overproof whiskey with spices, botanicals, and seasonal fruit, but Nate Shuman conjures a smoky sense of place with the distinctive barbecue bitters he makes at Proof & Provision, a cocktail bar tucked in the basement of Atlanta's historic Georgian Terrace Hotel. Shuman adds a few dashes to a wickedly alluring rye-and-mescal-based concoction he calls the Plaza en Fuego, but you can also use his secret-sauce elixir in a manhattan or anywhere brown spirits reign. (Pro tip: The added hit of smoke and spice also works great in a Bloody Mary.) Take a look at how Shuman does it and you begin to understand the beauty of bitters—something like seasoning for a cocktail.

SMOKY BITTERS

2 tbsp. **black peppercorns**

1 tbsp. **cumin seeds**

1 tbsp. **yellow mustard seeds**

1 tbsp. **black mustard seeds**

2 tbsp. **espresso beans**

2 dried **chipotle peppers**

4 **sun-dried tomato** halves

15 tbsp. **dried oregano**

1 fistful **thyme** (stems and all)

3 tbsp. **gentian root**

4 **bay leaves**

Zest of 3 **oranges**

Zest of 3 **grapefruit**

750 ml **grain alcohol**

IN A MEDIUM SAUCEPAN, toast the black peppercorns and the cumin seeds until aromatic. Briefly toast the mustard seeds. Using a spice grinder or a mortar and pestle, crush the peppercorn, cumin, mustard seeds, and espresso beans. Combine this dry mix with all the remaining ingredients in a mason jar and shake well. Let the mixture macerate for 10 days (shake well daily for best results), strain thoroughly through cheesecloth, and start barbecuing some cocktails. The bitters don't need to be stored in the refrigerator, but they're best used within a year for maximum flavor.

WHAT IS BOURBON ANYWAY?

NO SPIRIT IS MORE iconic below the Mason-Dixon Line than the brown-hued elixir known as bourbon. It would be a challenge to find a Southerner without a good bourbon story. If it's not your libation of choice, your father drank it, or your mother cooked with it, simply calling it whiskey, or your grandfather had a secret eggnog recipe calling for bourbon poured with a heavy hand. But while many of us are well acquainted with the taste of bourbon, misinformation abounds as to what, exactly, it is.

It's true that all bourbon is whiskey, but not all whiskey is bourbon. Whiskey is simply an alcoholic spirit distilled from a fermented grain mash. To qualify as bourbon under American law, however, it must be distilled in the United States from a mash that is at least 51 percent corn. The rest can be rye, wheat, or barley, each of which brings its own nuance to the blend.

Bourbon also must be aged in new charred-oak barrels. And while plain old bourbon can age for any amount of time, liquor labeled as *straight* bourbon must have passed at least two years in the wood. These days, you'll find some aged for much longer. The oldest bourbon in the venerable Pappy Van Winkle line sits in barrels for twenty-three years, losing roughly fifty of its fifty-three gallons to evaporation along the way.

You'll notice that nothing in the law says that bourbon must come from

Kentucky, where it originated in the late eighteenth century, though around 95 percent of the country's bourbon still does. Distillers prize the Bluegrass State's limestone-filtered water. Important, too, are its defined seasons. As temperatures swing from swampy to frigid, barreled whiskey expands and contracts in and out of the oak, mellowing significantly and absorbing flavor.

You may also have heard the term "Tennessee whiskey," a moniker used by whiskey giants Jack Daniel's and George Dickel. Those brands distinguish themselves with a method of charcoal filtration known as the Lincoln County Process.

But although they prefer to remain in a category of their own, they pass legal muster as bourbons, too.

So what's the right way to drink bourbon? "It's really just preference," says Pappy Van Winkle head Julian Van Winkle. "It's about how you like your whiskey." It's by no means a sin to dilute a higher-proof whiskey with a splash of water, which helps to cut the alcoholic burn and open up its subtler flavors. (An ice cube or two can accomplish the same thing.) Van Winkle even sometimes accents a glass with a twist of lemon. So do what tastes good to you. Bourbon is supposed to be fun, after all—that's why we love it.

THREE ODES TO BOURBON

THE GREAT WALKER PERCY'S classic 1975 essay on bourbon praises the aesthetic of swilling that "little explosion of Kentucky U.S.A. sunshine . . . and the hot bosky bite of Tennessee summertime." Per Percy, "Bourbon does for me what the piece of cake did for Proust." With this in mind, three modern Southern writers spent a little quality time with a bottle or two to meditate on the spirit of the South.

SIPPING WHISKEY

BY ROY BLOUNT, JR.

You should never drink whiskey alone, unless there's nobody else around and you have research to do involving drinking whiskey—in this case, trying to get to the bottom of why I like whiskey so much. But not to the bottom of any of the three bottles involved in this research. If I were to reach bottle bottom and enlightenment simultaneously, or concurrently, I might not feel the same way about my conclusions, or even remember them, in the morning.

My research so far: a sip of Jack Daniel's, a sip of Wild Turkey, and a sip of Bulleit Bourbon, which is new to me. They are all good. Plenty good enough. I like those single-malt scotches and special reserve bourbons, but unless somebody else is serving them, they cost too much for me to enjoy.

One thing about whiskey is, it has so many great names. Old Overholt, the Famous Grouse, Black Bush, Heaven Hill, Tullamore Dew. And let's face it, it's what they drink in cowboy movies. You don't see white hats or black hats tossing back shots of vodka or rum or taking a bottle of pinot grigio to the table.

Usually, when I drink whiskey it's Jack Daniel's, Tennessee sipping whiskey. I just had a sip from the bottle, and it was good. But you know what Jack Daniel's doesn't have that Wild Turkey and this Bulleit Bourbon do? A cork. A cork is a great thing in a whiskey bottle for the pleasure of pulling it out. Let's see if I can spell the sound: *f-toong*. That's if you pull it straight out. If you give it a little twist as you pull it, there's a squeak—no, a chirp, a tweet even—that drowns out the *f* and even the *t*. Interesting. That never really registered with me before. Sort of *squeeoong*.

A good thing about whiskey is that you can drink more of it than you can martinis. "Razor-blade soup" is what somebody once called a good dry martini, and I enjoy one (not flavored with chocolate or whatever—bleh!), but two of them is about a half of one too much for me. I can't remember ever doing anything rousing or having any very interesting conversation after two martinis. On the other hand, I can have two or three whiskeys, occasionally (never more than six or seven nights a week), and get relaxed rather than poleaxed. I can even write. See? Drive, no, but there's no way you can run over anybody while writing.

Maybe I should work up something to say when I take a sip, or, okay, a slug, of whiskey. In *Easy Rider*, Jack Nicholson says this: "NICK . . . NICK . . . NICK, ff ff, INDIANS!" That's a little too elaborate for me. Not to mention ethnically insensitive. Here's to everybody! Whoops! Or, no, this is more cowboy: Whoopee!

I like Wild Turkey, and this Bulleit isn't at all bad, and, by the way, the Bulleit comes in a flask-shaped bottle that is pretty cool. Jack Daniel's, however, is just 80 proof, whereas the Bulleit is 90, and this Wild Turkey I have is—whoa—101. So you can drink more of the Jack Daniel's. How much more? Well, I never said I could drink and do percentages.

Love those corks, though. Too much. I've pulled them so many times now tonight, trying to decide which one has the better tone, that they've lost their music. Kinda sad. I've worn them down. They're not tight anymore.

I am, though. Just to the point where I'm feeling sorry for corks and have forgotten what exactly I was researching. But I enjoyed it. Do I live near here?

RESPECTING RESERVE

BY JOHN T. EDGE

When I was in my late twenties, living in Atlanta, my friend Nelson Ross taught me the value of better bourbon. But he did it in an ass-backward way.

Nelson was keen on Blanton's, the first single-barrel bourbon. He liked the squat bottle. He liked the horse that pranced atop the stopper. And he liked the whiskey within, secure in the knowledge that his bottle was not filled from the spigot of an industrial sluice silo. Instead, Nelson's bottle of Blanton's was traceable to

a single charred oak barrel that, when the distiller tapped the bung in preparation for a bottling run, bloomed with scents of toffee and fig—the scents, in short, of fine bourbon.

Problem was, Nelson only drank Blanton's on special occasions. And on those special occasions he drank Blanton's from eggcups—actual eggcups—fashioned out of pickled eggs, sold by his favorite barkeep.

The idea was almost ingenious: With a pocketknife, cut a pickled egg across the midsection. Scoop the yolk from each half, taking care not to tear the white. Pour a dram of bourbon in each cup and swirl to dislodge any clinging yolk matter. Fill the eggcups in the manner of shot glasses and gulp.

For the longest time, I associated good bourbon with a sulfurous back end. Truth is, in those days bourbon was nothing more than drunkard's fuel. Blanton's was wasted on my friends and me because, well, we were wasted when we drank it. Not freshmen-in-college wasted, but sufficiently addled by longnecks that, by the time someone pulled out a pocketknife, we couldn't discern the difference between top shelf and bottom rung.

I'm now in my forties. And I still pitch a drunk now and again. But I don't drink Blanton's. Good as it may be, Blanton's comes with too much olfactory baggage.

I've upgraded my liquor cabinet—and my china cabinet. Now when I reach for a better bourbon, I pour a crystal rocks glass of twenty-year-old Pappy Van Winkle Family Reserve, the pride of Van Winkle men for three generations. After twenty summers in oak, Pappy, a wheated Kentucky whiskey, conjures a cognac gone country, which is to say the nose is soft, tobacco-sweet, almost floral, but the back end still kicks like a corn-fed mule.

No, I'm not going effete on you, Nelson. It's just that I've come to respect bourbon as more than a mere buzz catalyst. I've come to appreciate the heft of a razor-lipped tumbler, sloshing with amber liquid. I've come to believe that—forgive me—while eggs and whiskey can mix, that doesn't mean they should.

Proud to Drink American

BY CHEF JOHN CURRENCE

I grew up in New Orleans, a town of birthright drinkers where cocktail history is debated like sport and your drink choice is defining. By the age of twenty-two I considered myself light-years ahead of my North Carolina college friends, and had even chosen an unsung import as my poison—Jameson Irish Whiskey. Painfully, I believed I understood my choice and, worse, thought it made a profound statement about the torture that I, like James Joyce, was suffering in life. Hubris, as it turns out, comes with a price tag, a lesson I was force-fed at a Scottish pub called Saucy Mary's, on the Isle of Skye, during the summer of 1988.

Little can match the humiliation of marching into a Scotsman's pub and proudly ordering an Irish whiskey. I was, it turns out, just that dumb. What I learned from that night was that there is an austere ethnocentricity surrounding whiskey, and to understand it you must first respect it. Twenty years later, I still feel the sting of the tongue-lashing I took from that particular gin-blossomed Highlander for my wrongheadedness: "If ye ehver spek ta meh like that aggen en mi own place, laddie, I'll toss ye owt on yer fookin' arse."

After my moment of whiskey clarity at Saucy Mary's, I became, out of shame, a Scotch drinker. Johnnie Walker Black was my brand of choice, and by my late twenties I'd gotten where I believed I had no tolerance for inferior whiskeys. Analysis of the single malts' subtleties bored me, and I found discussion of the flavor profiles of different varieties brutally tedious. Johnnie Walker fit as well as a trusted pair of boots, and like broken-in leather, it felt good and carried me where I needed to go. But more important, if I was civilized enough to appreciate the King's Whisky, what else was there to discuss? It was just that simple.

Lessons being one thing, my epiphany came at a liquor store in Richmond, Virginia, several years later. On a January duck hunting trip, a good friend was espousing the nuances of different barrel-aging techniques of a particular Scotch when I began to feel the "Isle of Skye shame" again: Here we were celebrating the Scots' triumphs at the still when for the last two hundred years our own countrymen had been laboring over a formidable American spirit of their own. The hollows of Appalachia are home to generations of bourbon, rye, and corn whiskey distillation, and I realized I'd never really stopped to give American whiskey due consideration. It was the beginning of a dangerous passion for me.

That passion has since grown into obsession. I have sipped and studied my way through every distillery I can find, both licensed and illicit, and have even dabbled a little in production. But where the rubber meets the road is where simple enjoyment gives rise to a profound understanding of who our people are, where they have been, and what they have endured. In this sense, sipping a good glass of bourbon is a bit like tasting the history of the American South. Bourbon making, like other great traditions, has survived the Civil War, Prohibition, segregation, and civil rights, and quality has prospered as a result of the hardship. Today American distillers are making hooch that stands tall with that of their European counterparts.

I proudly drink American now, and I choose bourbon over anything else because I love its sweetness and the flavor of the grains. But I enjoy it because it speaks of the South and a respect for our traditions. And while I don't necessarily wince when someone approaches my bar and orders an Irish whiskey, I certainly understand my Scottish barkeep's indignation a hell of a lot better.

Part Four

SPORTING & ADVENTURE

WISDOM OF THE FIELD

BY GUY MARTIN

*I*T WOULD SURELY MAKE US BRAVER AND FINER PEOPLE IF WE LIVED OUR LIVES AS FARMERS OR AS FISHERMEN, BECAUSE THEIR WHEREWITHAL IS IN THE GROUND AND IN THE WATER, ABSOLUTELY AT RISK AND IN PLAY. TO THIS DAY, THE KEY TO THE SOUTH'S WORK AND TO ITS PLAY IS ITS PROXIMITY TO THAT GIFT OF NATURE—WHETHER WE MEAN THE DOVE SHOOTS BUILT ON THE CORN HARVEST, OR THE MASSIVE MIGRATION OF THE WATERFOWL DOWN THROUGH THE ARKANSAS, MISSISSIPPI, AND LOUISIANA WETLANDS, OR THE BIG APRIL PUSH OF THE ZEUS-LIKE TARPON INTO THE SHALLOW WATER OF THE FLORIDA KEYS.

With so much natural bounty so close upon us comes the duty to hone the skills to address it, and that's an amazing bit of good fortune felt in every corner of the region. From Curaçao to the Kentucky bluegrass, the unruly mass of aquatic and terrestrial fertility—and the climates and microclimates that support it—is how the how-to-ness of the South came to be. Each place has its vocabulary of skill. South

Louisiana crabbers know where and how to pull up what they call the jimmies, the luscious blues that are immediately flown to the best chefs in the nation; on the vast flats of the Abacos, the legendary guide Joe Cleare could spot a tailing bonefish at 150 yards; in Jasper, Alabama, Jimmy Fikes can make you a hunting knife with which you can breast a pheasant or with which you can shave.

The immediacy of nature also influences the custom, the social approach to the soft march of the seasons and its rituals. Southerners think nothing—or put another way, think *everything*—of dove and quail dinners, crawfish boils, wild-turkey Thanksgivings, redfish and pompano feasts, bream and crappie fish fries. The home cook creates these things with an unsurpassed level of generosity and style. Harvesttime is harvesttime, and—again, luckily, because of the geophysical accident of bounty—it's pretty much all the time, in every nook and cranny of the region.

My grandfather's farm was in town, not outside it. This is nothing new, but it's a lovely peculiarity of small Southern towns that there are houses on a nominal street in back of which are barns, some pasture, and random shambling, busted outbuildings left over from the nineteenth century. In my family's case this compound was extended: Facing the street were my grandfather's and great-grandfather's houses, behind which were two servants' houses (one abandoned), a barn, a smokehouse, and twenty-five acres with a creek for my wild little quarter horse and my brother Joe's strange, stubborn Shetland pony. Our grandfather had just stopped having cattle out back, as I understood from the many cow piles I stumbled through as I tried to bridle my horse while she skipped blithely away in his huge pasture.

Such an environment demands skill. My horse was given to me unbroken, so I quickly set about earning a degree at the university of equine malfeasance, getting kicked, bitten, and thrown while having to master the many fine tricks of bridling and saddling a large animal that didn't want to play with me so much as she wanted to fight. When our parents moved us to the country, we began living our lives alongside the many great snakes in the woods and creeks behind our house. Not a summer day passed without a copperhead or a king or a cottonmouth appearing at some turn in our play. Tiring of shooting them or letting the dogs have at them, my brother Carl began collecting them, then moved on to squirrels, rabbits, and finally graduated to a four-foot iguana, which he let roam freely in the bedroom I shared with him.

I never understood how Carl got the damn thing, but anything like that usually came from what I knew to be the insane beach-dwelling hucksters of the state of Florida. Quite a few people in the state of Alabama, however, would not set foot in our room after the iguana moved in, including our mother. The iguana wandered implacably across my schoolbooks, and often across me, and at night he'd hang by his claws high on the silk curtains, thinking his special Paleolithic monster thoughts, backlit by the moon. It was an excellent primer on how to live with a dragon.

The homeland holds yet another splendid teaching gift: So much of the South is broken in the most challenging way, broken by the sheer effort of being and working, "wallered out," as a farmer friend once jauntily described the hitch behind her favorite tractor. It was plowing time, and all the farms around her in Morgan County, Alabama, were in the same fix. Things broken in the previous harvest had not quite been mended. That late in the tilling season, the welders were booked like battlefield surgeons.

A grandee's daughter educated at private schools, this girl had never held the roar of an oxyacetylene torch or the big searing snap of a nine-inch electrode in her hands. But, full of what I'll call the best sort of farmer grit, she headed out that day to learn how to do it.

DOVE MOVES

THE SEPTEMBER DOVE opener is like the Southern rush week you never outgrow: part theater, part sporting event, and all spectacle. It's also the time when your prowess as a scattergunner is easy to see, both in the number of birds in your bag and the number of smoking shells at your feet. Here's how to boost your percentages.

1. GET ON YOUR FEET: Shooting a shotgun well requires pivoting through the shot—which you can't do while affixed to a bucket. The more shots you take while standing, the more shots you'll make.

2. FOOT THE BILL: If you're a right-handed shooter, point your left foot toward the airspace where the bird's beak will be when you pull the trigger. Lefties, point the right foot.

3. KEEP YOUR HEAD DOWN: As the bird approaches, keep the dove just visible beneath your hat brim. Quick movements and a big shiny face will tip your hand.

4. LOOK IT IN THE EYE: Focus on the bird's eye—literally. That'll keep you from being distracted by other doves cartwheeling into view and will establish a line of motion you'll track with the shotgun.

5. WAIT FOR IT: Keep the gun low and parallel to the ground until you're ready to shoot. Mount the gun by bringing

the stock to your cheek, without moving your head, and swing the muzzle to track the bird in one smooth movement. Concentrate on maintaining focus on the bird.

6. LEAD WELL: On long crossing shots, swing the muzzle ahead of the bird and move the bead at the same speed as the dove. If you've practiced, you'll know how much to lead. If you miss, double the lead on the next shot. On closer incomers, sweep the muzzle through the bird and pull the trigger when the dove disappears.

7. SWING AWAY: After the shot, keep the muzzle moving and keep your head down. A good follow-through not only increases your odds of connecting but keeps you loose and fluid for a follow-up shot or a try at a double.

FALL OFF A HORSE

HERE'S A CERTAINTY. Spend a decent amount of time in the saddle and eventually something will go wrong, usually leaving you on the ground in a cloud of dust. The best riders, seasoned by experience, know how to fall so, it is hoped, they can climb back on the horse with little more than a bruised ego. Bill Green is one of these riders.

"When you know you're falling off a horse, don't fight the fall," says Green, a lifelong horseman who serves as master of the hounds at South Carolina's Middleton Hunting Club. Green has spent years riding through the thickest Southern woods at breakneck speed. There are all manner of reasons a person might exit the saddle—an errant branch, an unprepared rider, an upset horse—and he has experienced all of them.

"When you're going down, all you should worry about is protecting your head and neck," Green says. To avoid complications, kick your feet out of the stirrups—if they have not slipped out already—and let go of the reins. Hold your limbs close to your body, gently. Though your first instinct might be to stick an arm out to break your fall, a hard fall will break a stiff arm. Relax your muscles and roll off the side of the horse, aiming to land as far from the animal as possible. You want to tumble—not thud—when you hit, Green says.

What happens next depends on the horse. "Some horses, you come off and they'll stop right with you," Green says. "If you know the horse, and you two have worked as a team, it will know to do that. But some horses will run right off and leave you." If you are intact enough to scramble back to your feet, and the horse has settled down enough to approach, put a hand on its flank and take the reins as quickly as possible. Assess whether you can get back to riding or need to call it a day, and proceed accordingly.

A TRUE SOUTHERN HORSE

Here in the South, we have a riding culture that stretches back centuries. And at the very beginning of that history sits one little breed that has been all but forgotten by most of the equestrian world: South Carolina's Marsh Tacky, a stocky horse descended from the animals brought to the South by sixteenth-century Spanish explorers.

For generations, Tackies ran semi-wild along the Southern coast, where locals valued them for their stamina and their ability to navigate tangled swamps. But the Marsh Tacky went out of fashion in the mid-twentieth century, following the rise of the automobile. And because many coastal Southerners viewed Tackies as little more than mangy plantation strays, they made little effort to keep the storied breed alive. By 2006, when members of the American Livestock Breeds Conservancy traveled to South Carolina to investigate the state of the Marsh Tacky, they identified just one hundred or so still in existence. That number has since increased, thanks to a renewed interest in the breed's history, but the horse remains critically endangered.

TICK TRICKS

DEER TICKS MAY get all the attention—they carry Lyme disease, which can result in everything from short-term fever and headaches to chronic joint problems—but in the South, the ones that matter are those little brown bastards often called wood ticks. And if you're out in the wild, they're out to get you. These buggers are officially known as lone star ticks (*Amblyomma americanum* to you scientists), but, geographically, they're found not just in Texas but in every Southern state. On you, geographically, they're usually found in more intimate places. Their eight wriggling legs, that pinhead speck of roach-colored shell, and the little white splotch—the "lone star"—on the females' backs make these ticks all the more revolting, and most

Southern kids will have heard rumors that they sometimes dig in near your spine and secrete deadly toxins. Those rumors are true. Thousands of Webelos die this way every year, but it's all covered up.

Okay, not really. But when you find one dug in, you of course want it off immediately, though it can sometimes be hard to get sage guidance from any equally hapless and infested companions. There always seems to be somebody far too eager to lean in and hold a smoldering cigarette or something similarly hot close to your flesh, compelling the tick to let go and retreat—but, according to one strand of folklore, not before vomiting into your bloodstream as a final act of revenge. Everybody knows you're not supposed to just grab and yank. Do that and the thing's head will break off, festering until it resembles a subcutaneous waterlogged raisin and hurts you with a special kind of hurt. And slathering a tick with insect repellent doesn't feel good or work. They're not insects; they're arachnids. They don't give a damn.

Fortunately, there are more experienced folks about, and they often have good tips for handling things like this. (Such as killing chiggers, or "red bugs," by painting over—and suffocating—them with clear fingernail polish.) One hoary tick-removal method instructs you to grasp the body with fingernails or tweezers and then slowly, carefully, twist it counter-clockwise (not clockwise) until it comes loose. Then, of course, you're to place the invader on a rock or a board and smush it with another rock.

This technique works fine if you keep things slow and careful, but it turns out the counterclockwise bit isn't necessary—just more misinformation. According to the latest science, though, you should take some tweezers, grab the tick's head (not its body) as close to the skin as possible, and pull straight out. The smushing part still holds up.

TAKE YOUR BEST SHOT

BY DAVID E. PETZAL

ALTHOUGH I'M a card-carrying Yankee, I've spent a great deal of time in the South and can testify that if I wanted to live there and gain social acceptance, I would need to know how to tell a story, put on a pig pull, pick the hell out of a guitar, and shoot good. This last may seem an odd addition to the list, but the fact is that, below the Mason-Dixon, skill with firearms has long been venerated, and I'm here to tell you the two secrets of becoming proficient—or better—with a gun.

A friend of mine once said, "All the really good shots I know have the nervous systems of serpents." Serpents don't worry about whether they'll look stupid or inept if they can't hit what they aim at. They probably don't think about very much at all. Oh, they may think, "Pickup truck make me flat" or "Don't bite setter because owner has gun," but it probably doesn't go beyond that. Good shots, like serpents, think about nothing.

If you're at a dove shoot with people watching you, for example, you'll come to the (correct) conclusion that it's now impossible to hit a dove with a charge of shot. Because you're thinking that you look like an oaf, your brain will short-circuit your nervous system, your hand-eye coordination will go elsewhere, and you'll slink from the field like a whipped cur.

However, if you master the Way of the Reptile, your brain will not even consider such questions, and you will shoot as the serpent strikes, Grasshopper.

The other secret is practice. I don't mean go out once in a while and shoot casually.

I mean go out a lot and shoot until there's a pool of your blood on the ground.

I mentioned guitar playing earlier. I myself was only a proficient amateur, but I played with professionals, and the differences between them and me were talent—they had a lot more than I did—and the amount of practice they put in. They played compulsively. They played all the time. One of them, who went on to win a Grammy or two, once spent four hours on the toilet simultaneously combating intestinal travail and working on some hot licks.

You may be one of those rare and gifted people who can pick up a gun cold and hit with it, but most likely you're not. If that's so, buy a ton of ammo and head to the range and shoot, and as you do so, think about absolutely nothing.

TROUT OF
THE SOUTH

THE BROOK TROUT is one of the South's most treasured game fish, and these fish live in the most beautiful places—namely cool mountain streams burbling under a shade-giving canopy. Their wild running grounds also ensure that any angling usually requires at least some basic orienteering and a willingness to cover some ground. Tom Sadler, a guide for the Mossy Creek Fly Fishing shop, in Virginia's Shenandoah Valley, is a brook trout junkie. His mantra when it comes to finding the best fishing for these precious jewels of the southeastern Appalachians is a simple one: "Instead of fighting the crowds, fight the underbrush."

Before a brookie jaunt, Sadler sits down with his most handy tool: a DeLorme map. ("I like maps better than a GPS," he says. "GPS devices have batteries, and those can fail.") On the map, Sadler goes straight to a well-known brook trout stream, such as, say, Virginia's Rapidan River. "Then I look for the feeder streams, those thin blue lines, and see where they go," he says. One can also look for these lines in nearly every national or state-owned property in the southeastern mountains. "If you find streams that are in or near the headwaters of a river, chances are they'll have brook trout."

And if they do, these unpressured fish are apt to take any reasonable offerings.

"Pheasant-tail nymphs, Royal Wulffs, or any of your go-to flies should work," Sadler says. But he cautions that the intrepid brookie angler has to manage expectations. "Don't forget that when chasing brook trout, half the fun is finding them."

THREE ESSENTIAL FLIES

Brook trout will bite all sorts of flies when they're hungry, making them an ideal target. The effectiveness of specific patterns will vary by season (check the fly shop nearest to your stream if you have the chance), but here are three go-to flies worth seeking out.

PARACHUTE ADAMS: This wildly effective version of the classic Adams fly will serve you just as well in Montana as it will in east Tennessee.

ROYAL WULFF: Try one of these if you're fishing in fast and turbulent water, particularly in the springtime. Later in the season, switch over to more subdued relatives like the Rusty Wulff or the Grey Wulff.

WOOLLY BUGGER: This fly is a style rather than a specific pattern, and it comes in a range of colors. Tie on a drab black or olive green variety when fishing the narrow streams of the mountain South.

OLD BLADE, NEW BITE

ARKANSAS KNIFE MAKER James Crowell knows a thing or two about putting an edge on a hunk of steel. A certified master bladesmith, Crowell is also a past winner of the annual World Championship Cutting Competition, where knife wielders perform such varied tasks as chopping through a two-by-four and slicing through a dangling inch-thick rope in a single stroke.

While Crowell uses a combination of methods to arrive at an edge he deems *sharp*, the good news, he says, is that most of us need only an old-fashioned sharpening stone to whip our blades into shape.

To begin, apply a light coating of honing oil to the stone. (Crowell prefers Norton India or Arkansas stones.) As metal is worn away from the knife, the oil will help float away the particles. After that, the key is to maintain a consistent angle as you push the blade across the surface. A good angle for general use is about 20 degrees. Start near the handle and push with firm pressure as if you are trying to slice a sliver off the top of the stone. If you're sharpening a large blade, it may be helpful to put the stone in a vise and use both hands to guide your knife.

Another trick Crowell recommends is to color the cutting edge of the blade with a marker. The ink will wear away as you sharpen, allowing you to see exactly where the blade is making contact with the stone.

Variations in the line mean changes in your sharpening angle. "What you're looking for is a smooth line of even width," he says. After a few strokes, switch hands and repeat the process on the other side. A dull knife will take several repetitions.

One word of caution: Sharpening with a stone takes practice. Don't try it out with your daddy's vintage Randall. But when you get it right, you'll know. "Once you cut with something really sharp," Crowell says, "you'll never forget it."

BE A BETTER DERBY BETTOR

THERE'S NO HYPERBOLE in calling the Kentucky Derby the greatest horse race of them all, and it's only beaten out by Mardi Gras for oldest and wildest cultural institution in the South. Unlike the Belmont and the Preakness, the legs that follow it in the U.S. Triple Crown, Louisville's "most exciting two minutes in sports" have been run annually without interruption since 1875—and have arguably seen horse racing's most heroic triumphs and tragedies. And that includes those of hopeful bettors.

The man who is known—also without hyperbole—as the greatest horse-race handicapper in the world now goes by the pseudonym Mr. Black. Why? After a spate of news stories about his racetrack successes in the early aughts, he was "relentlessly hounded by the crazies," who cyberstalked him and called him at home in the middle of the night, begging for any scrap of information to help them crack the code. Thankfully, Mr. Black decided to let us in on four key secrets to betting the Derby. And while none of these are foolproof, he says, they can help you play with your money less foolishly.

1. DON'T BET THE FAST STARTERS: "The Derby has a lot of these horses. The reason is that a lot of owners enter a horse in the race for vanity reasons. I've seen a guy run a horse that had never been over seven furlongs! [The Derby is ten.] He did it because he thought it was his last chance to have a Derby horse. These speed horses run quickly at the start and tire at the end. For this reason, the Derby tends to favor horses coming from the back. Check out the times the horses ran in races leading up to the Derby."

2. LOOK FOR A HOT HORSE WITH GOOD ODDS: "You want a horse that's coming into the Derby off some good races.

The 2012 winner, I'll Have Another, had done well in both starts before the Derby and was still around twenty to one. Money can be made here."

3. TRAINERS AND JOCKEYS ARE OVERRATED: "You don't need a trainer with Derby experience to win the race, and some jockeys are overbet because of who they are. The hype exceeds reality. You have better odds with the less well known."

4. BET HORSES THAT START ON THE OUTSIDE: "Historically, the Derby is run with twenty horses. They don't have a twenty-horse starting gate. They have one for the first fourteen horses and an auxiliary gate on the outside for horses fifteen to twenty. The auxiliary gate horses seem to get through the starting scrum with greater ease."

NET RESULTS

LEARNING HOW TO throw a cast net is a rite of passage for those growing up in the coastal South. Not only can you catch your own bait, you can snag a shrimp dinner, too. When it comes to the technique, though, it's all about burgers and bananas. A burger, in the argot of cast netters, is a perfect throw, one that opens up the net in a complete circle before it hits the water. A banana is a cast that flies through the air like, well, a banana. With no coverage over the water, the net has little chance of catching anything on its way to the bottom.

Peter Brown has been throwing burgers since he was six years old. A fishing guide based in Charleston, South Carolina, Brown learned the skill from his grandfather. Thirty years ago, most cast nets were handmade from cotton or nylon and were things of beauty. They were also damn heavy when wet, making them pretty tough for a young boy to cast. These days cast nets are made from monofilament and are much lighter. And there are as many methods to throw them as there are to cook shrimp. If you're new to the game, a five-foot net with a half-inch mesh is a good size to start with. Brown, who has a variety of nets, depending on whether he's after shrimp, menhaden, or mullet, still prefers to cast the way he was taught as a child.

As for finding shrimp, there's no better time than the fall, when the season's shrimp have had time to grow into eating size. Look for them on a falling tide as the water leaves the marsh grass. "If you can find a deep pocket on a mud flat, it'll be loaded with shrimp," Brown says.

Once you have a bucketful, the choice of how to cook them is all yours: boiled, fried, grilled, or, of course, ground up in shrimp burgers.

CAST MASTER

1. PUT THE LOOP AROUND YOUR LEFT WRIST (reverse all directions if you're a lefty) and coil the line in your hand. With your left hand, grab the net about six inches below the horn (the plastic ring at the top of the net).

2. GRAB THE LEAD LINE (the line at the base of the net) and place it between your teeth. Do not put the lead weights in your mouth. With your right hand, reach down an arm's length and grab the lead line. The bottom of the net should be just above the boat deck.

3. YOU'RE READY. Gently turn in a counterclockwise motion and then forcefully reverse your swing to send the net flying forward, lifting your arms slightly to give it some height.

4. AS THE NET BEGINS TO OPEN, release the lead line from your mouth and the net from both hands. After the net hits the water, allow it to sink to the bottom, then pull the main line in with sharp tugs.

THE FASTEST WAY TO START A FIRE

IN THE RURAL SOUTH few folks need an artificial fire log or a cup of diesel fuel to get a fire roaring. Usually a single match is applied strategically to a rudimentary pile of branches, and before long flames leap toward the sky. This is neither magic nor skill. The secret is fatwood, a natural fire starter that abounds in Southern forests.

Fatwood (or lighter wood) began its life as a pine tree that was eventually felled by man or toppled in a storm. With the roots still pumping sap into the stump, the wood becomes saturated with high concentrations of resin. This resin, which is also used to make turpentine, is highly flammable.

Locating these stumps takes a little practice, but as a general rule a fatwood stump won't be soft or crumbly. Not sure? Give the stump a thump with your boot; if it crumbles, move on. Once you find a weathered and ancient-looking stump that stands up to the boot test, pull out a knife and carve off a splinter of wood. The interior portion of the splinter should be sticky and glossy, and smell like a fresh-cut pine. With your stump located, hack your fatwood into chunks and cart it out of the woods. At home you can make tinder shavings or cut pieces about as long as a chopstick and twice as wide. Think of them as matches on steroids . . . a lot of steroids. Whatever your campfire technique—tepee, log cabin, mixed, freestyle—fatwood is guaranteed to make it work, even in the rain. And it's a whole lot safer than that cup of diesel fuel.

GRAB A FROG

A FROG LEG CAN have as much meat as a drumstick off your average chicken, and cooked right, whether deep-fried or sautéed, it's just as good eating too. Which is why people all over the South have been gigging the critters (that is, spearing them out of the water with a trident or something similar) since God knows when.

If you've ever hunted bullfrogs yourself, chances are it was using the gig method. And while to many of us that's pretty much the apotheosis of Southern country cool, compared with hand grabbing, it's sissy work. Deep in Louisiana's Atchafalaya Basin, frog hunters crouch like jaguars on the bow of a crawfish boat while a buddy works a spotlight and a motor tiller to get close, close, and closer.

Caught in the bright beam, the bullfrogs remain bug-eyed and motionless, as if watching the grim reaper coming for their squalid souls. Once close enough, said frog hunters grab the frogs one-handed, arm in the swamp to the shoulder, with the other hand gripping the boat gunwale as if they might be dragged across the River Styx.

Watch them at work and you'll learn that the only way to approach frog grabbing is with all-in commitment. It's not a jab. It's a full-on roundhouse, pinching ol' Galump with thumb and fingers as you drive the slippery amphibian into the mud and muck. Once extracted, the frogs go into a wet burlap sack, so you can hit the hay when you're done and worry about cleaning them later.

OUR NATURAL WONDERS

THEY SAY THE Appalachian Mountains are about nine times older than those stultifyingly spectacular Himalayas. Some weathering is to be expected when you're that ancient. What the South's cardinal peaks have lost in height and mass, however, they've gained in subtlety and a deep, mysterious majesty. It's why they tend to pop up the most in conversations about the natural beauty of our region. But if you know what to look for, you'll find we've got plenty of other flavors of sublime wilderness out there to be experienced. Consider this a checklist.

1. LONGLEAF PINE SAVANNAS: With straight-trunked trees towering over expansive meadows of wire grass and wildflowers, longleaf pine savannas are one of the most biologically rich habitats in North America. Few virgin stands remain, but more and more landowners are restoring the quail-rich woodlands.

Where to see: The 300,000-acre Red Hills region between Thomasville, Georgia, and Tallahassee, Florida.

2. BARRIER ISLANDS: Ranging from tiny ribbons of sand to islands measured by the square mile, barrier islands buffer the Southern coast from storm tides and provide critical wildlife habitat to sea turtles, shorebirds, and even rare beach mice.

Where to see: At 26,000 acres, Georgia's Ossabaw Island ranks among the largest of the Atlantic barrier islands.

3. CYPRESS SWAMPS: With their trunks sunk deep into primordial muck and crowns shattered and blackened by a few centuries' worth of storms, cypress swamps are as Southern gothic as any landscape in Dixie.

Where to see: Logging for cypress mulch is taking its toll on Gulf Coast cypress trees, but Louisiana's Atchafalaya Basin retains awe-inspiring stands.

4. PLAYAS: Ephemeral, paradoxical, phoenix-like in their ability to suddenly emerge from a parched landscape with a passing shower, playas are perhaps the most enigmatic of North American wetlands. These shallow, often circular freshwater wetlands are atomized across the Great Plains like azure coins flung across the land.

Where to see: The Texas panhandle from Lubbock north to the state line.

5. SOUTHERN APPALACHIAN BALDS: Capping high-elevation mountains in Tennessee, Virginia, North Carolina, and Georgia, these alpine grasslands attract vesper sparrows, broad-winged hawks, and happy hikers who ascend to the windswept crests for the best mountain views in the South.

Where to see: Tennessee's Roan Mountain State Park and Virginia's Grayson Highlands State Park.

RIVER CAMPING

FEW ADVENTURES HOLD the romantic allure of hitching a couple of bags to a small boat and heading down the river, Huck Finn–style. But plenty of soggy campers will tell you that it pays to know what you're getting into when paddling the Southern wild. Veteran guide Randy Holton, who has led runs down the South's Chattooga, Ocoee, Gauley, New, and Nantahala Rivers, has learned over the years what makes the difference between a successful expedition and a watery slog.

Before leaving the house, Holton says, do your homework. Study a river, paying special attention to its speed, depth, and steepness. The Chattooga, for example, has an ominous reputation but long stretches of relatively easy water that are perfect for overnight and multiday runs. The Ocoee, on the other hand, is basically a two-and-a-half-hour white-knuckle thrill ride. And be sure to keep abreast of current conditions. High water can transform easy stretches into rapids and can send a boat downstream twice as fast. On the other hand, if a river is at low summertime or drought levels, exposed rocks and sandbars can leave you high and dry. Ask around before you put in. "Local outfitters are usually very generous with their knowledge," Holton says, "even if you're not planning on traveling with them."

Whether a river is raging or mellow, always assume you'll get dunked and waterproof everything. Keep your gear in dry bags or, at the least, tightly sealed coolers, and make sure dry clothes are easily accessible. "It may be sunny and nice," adds Holton, "but the water can still be deadly cold. You can instantly go from being hot and dry to being at serious risk of hypothermia." And don't forget to keep some kind of fire starter in a waterproof container too.

When it comes time to bed down for the night, choose your campsite wisely. It's a safe bet that any barren patch of sand has been under water recently. An isthmus that is half forested upland and half sandbar might become an island on a rainy day. Any grassy site with trees is probably a good spot for a night's rest. After beaching your boat, be sure to tie it up; sudden river rises, particularly after summer storms, might run off with it otherwise. Same story if you're camping on a tidal river.

"One other thing," Holton says. "Don't rely on a GPS to know when it's time to take out. You should know what your takeout looks like from upstream. Otherwise, you can paddle right on by."

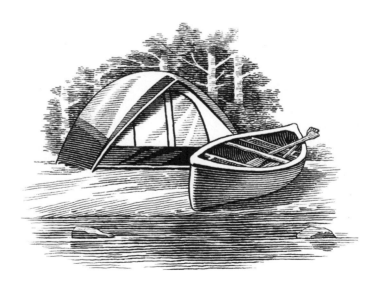

THE BLUEGILL MOON

LONG ABOUT WHEN the dogwoods fade, time and place conspire to usher in some of the finest, most accessible fishing in the South. The buzz starts building in late April at ponds and lakes all over the region: The bluegill spawn is near. The beloved panfish—as in flat, roundish, and perfect for your frying pan—is easy to catch, fun to fight, and good to eat. And bluegill fishing is a sport for Everyman. And every kid and grandmother. Pretty much everybody's a fan of the bluegill spawn.

Bluegill spawning beds appear overnight, it seems, like the tracks of some plodding beast, in the pond shallows or along the lakeshore: cream-colored craters the size of dinner plates, packed so tightly in places it's as if the mud bottom is honeycombed. Breathe deep. You can smell the fish. As the moon grows full in May, the bluegill spawn peaks. Fish move into the shallows to fan out their button-shaped beds. There can be scores in a space the size of a decent dog pen. With eggs in the nest, the 'gills ferociously defend their beds, like any good mama would.

You can catch them by dappling a cricket or a catalpa worm from a cane pole or dragging a grub-tipped spinner-bait through the beds, and there's not a thing wrong with either approach. But fly casting to bedding bluegills is so easy and so effective and so much fun that it's hard to pass up the long rod for anything else.

There's no hatch to match. You're throwing meat and potatoes to these panfish. A rubber spider or a tiny foam popper the color of candy corn will be slurped down in a nanosecond. Double the pleasure by tying a 24-inch dropper of light monofilament leader to the bend of a popper hook and arm this double whammy with a sinking black ant. Now you can fish the surface and dredge the bottom on the same cast, catching active feeders as well as subterranean bruisers skulking in the deeper beds.

If the resulting melee of cast-after-cast action wasn't so much fun, and if the spoils of your deception weren't so fine and tasty, you might reconsider such a one-sided fight. Instead, mark your calendar: The June full moon can be nearly as good.

NO-FAIL FRYING

There's a reason why the bluegill is called a panfish. Use your favorite fish batter (or try ours on page 35), and follow these rules to avoid soggy, burned, or undercooked fillets.

FILL YOUR CAST-IRON skillet about two-thirds of the way to the top with oil. That ensures an even fry without too much splatter.

HEAT THE OIL to 360 degrees, testing the temperature with a thermometer or a one-inch cube of bread—when the oil is ready, the bread should take about a minute to brown.

FRY THE BATTERED fillets on one side until golden, a few minutes, and then flip and fry the other side for the same amount of time. Adjust the time slightly for larger or smaller fish.

REMOVE WITH A slotted spoon, drain on a plate lined with paper towels, and dig in.

THROW A ROPE

CHANCES ARE YOUR livelihood doesn't depend on being able to successfully rope a steer. But lassoing the nearest fence post (or your rambunctious nephew) sure makes one heck of a party trick.

Kirk Bray, a Texas panhandle native, grew up in a rodeo family. He was a seasoned roper by grade school, ultimately heading to college on a rodeo scholarship. He's now president of the United States Team Roping Championships, which puts on roping events all over the country.

First, you'll need to find yourself a good lariat (any well-stocked saddle shop should carry one). "I would recommend that beginners look for a lightweight, limber rope," Bray says. The softer and smaller in diameter a rope is, the easier it is to throw. While cowboys once bought their ropes stiff and stretched them out around trees, most modern-day ropes can head straight from the shelf to the ranch.

When you're ready to throw, coil most of your rope in your left hand (or right, if you're left-handed), leaving about five feet free. Extend the loop at the end of the lariat (called the "catch loop") to a diameter of several feet. Grasp the loop and the rope together about a foot away from the *honda*, the sliding knot that makes the catch loop. You want the rope to lie across your palm, with your index finger extended along it. Make sure to keep a light touch. "Most beginners grip a rope like they're picking up a suitcase by the handle," Bray says.

With a loose wrist, spin the rope counterclockwise over your head to gain momentum. The unhurried cowboy might revolve the rope three to six times before releasing it. When you are ready to cast, pitch your arm forward and throw the catch loop, pointing at the target with your index finger. Let the rope glide through your hands. "You throw a rope kind of like you throw a baseball," Bray says. "You want to point to your target and follow through. The index finger helps with that."

Once you've hit your target, pull back with your left hand to tighten your hold. And keep in mind, when you hit everything but your target, that good roping, like any athletic skill, comes from lots and lots of practice.

FOR THE BIRD-WATCHERS

FROM THE TINY calliope hummingbird to the great blue heron, the South is home to a stunning array of avian diversity, offering crucial habitat for thousands of bird species and lying under countless migration flyways. So if a day outside with a pair of binoculars close at hand sounds like a day well spent, you're in the right place. Even if you're not a hard-core birder, chances are you'll see some very charismatic feathered friends. Here are five of the South's largest and most spectacular species.

1. AMERICAN OYSTERCATCHER: These striking black-and-white shorebirds are better than a foot tall, with a wingspan of nearly three feet and a long, intensely orange beak. It's this beak that really sets the oystercatcher apart, giving it the ability to hammer the shells of clams and oysters until they shatter or to pry them open with a finesse that makes lifelong oystermen jealous. In the South, oystercatchers can be found in salt marshes from Virginia clear around to Texas.

2. PILEATED WOODPECKER: Next to the huge and quite possibly extinct ivory-billed, the pileated is the biggest woodpecker in North America. At almost twenty inches long, with a thirty-inch wingspan, zebra-stripe face, and brilliant red crown feathers, it's a glorious bird. Pileateds peck trees

in a rapidly escalating jackhammer fashion, and their call is straight out of a Tarzan movie. They're found across much of eastern North America and are particularly fond of old Southern forests, and even old Southern suburbs, where mature trees hide the bugs and grubs they love.

3. MAGNIFICENT FRIGATEBIRD: These ornery birds are among the most distinctive creatures along Southern shores, with forked tails, wingspans of better than seven feet, and the ability to "lock" their wings and sleep in the air. To impress the ladies, a male will cock his head back and make drumming sounds with the large, inflatable red pouch on his neck. During their summer mating season, the iridescent magnificents, a.k.a. man-of-war birds, are easy to spot in the Florida Keys, where they nest and roost in mangroves. They're particularly common in the Dry Tortugas, off Key West, where they hover on afternoon thermals in dense packs.

4. WHOOPING CRANE: One of North America's greatest—but still perilous—conservation successes is the highly intelligent whooping crane, which stands up to five feet tall and has a wingspan of up to eight feet. Though mostly a brilliant white, these giant birds sport black wing tips and legs and a black-and-scarlet mask. Since 1941, they've recovered from a low point of sixteen birds to more than five hundred. During the winter months, after their 2,500-mile migration from Canada, you can see them along Gulf Coast salt-marsh shores, from White Lake, Louisiana, to Texas's Aransas National Wildlife Refuge. Florida sees another, smaller migratory population winter in the St. Marks and Chassahowitzka wildlife refuges, while one small flock lives year-round in the Kissimmee Prairie area.

5. BALD EAGLE: Not long ago, bald eagle sightings were all but unheard of in the South. By 1963, loss of habitat, *highly* illegal shooting, and rampant DDT poisoning of food sources had left only 487 wild nesting pairs of our great sea eagle in its native North America. But the Endangered Species Act and countless conservationists brought the nation's mascot back up to more than 11,000 pairs. Eagles mate for life and can be seen building their massive nests in pine trees across an increasingly broad, watery swath of the South, with key spots including Tennessee's Hiawassee Wildlife Refuge, South Carolina's ACE Basin, Louisiana's Lake Pontchartrain, Arkansas's Petit Jean State Park, and Florida's St. Johns River.

WRESTLE AN ALLIGATOR

FIRST, LET'S BE CLEAR, there's no good reason to wrestle an alligator unless you're showing off in front of a crowd. And if that's the case, may we suggest learning how to throw a lariat instead (see page 156). If you're still reading, you need to know alligator wrestling is not the knock-down, drag-out, tooth-and-nail sport that you might imagine. It is more akin to gymnastics than cage fighting, with graceful movements planned carefully and executed with precision. But though alligator wrestling may be more about spectacle than strength, it *is* genuinely dangerous.

Tim Williams is acutely aware of these perils. The Florida native began working at Orlando, Florida's Gatorland theme park shortly after returning from Vietnam. Today, he serves as the park's head gator wrestler. "A young guy asked me once, 'Hey, can you tell me if I'm doing it wrong?' And I said, 'You'll know.'"

If you want to wrestle a gator, Williams says, you'll have to start with a permit and some basic knowledge of crocodilian behavior. "The gator is instinctive. First, it wants to get away. Then, if that doesn't work, it wants to turn around and fight you. The gator does not have a lot of stamina, though, so after a while it gets tired."

Approach a gator from behind and grab hold of its tail. Pull the alligator out of the water by the tail. Then, in one swift movement, pull the alligator toward you and spring forward onto its back, planting your knees on each side of its body and your hands on its neck. Watch the tail, if you can. "A gator might hit you with its tail," Williams says, "and it will hurt. It can even break a bone. But like I tell my wrestlers, the back end will beat you and the front end will eat you."

Slide one hand up the gator's neck and use it to cover the eyes. The gator should calm down a little bit. Then, grab the mouth with your other hand. Hold tight. Pull the head up—not back, like you're going to break the neck, just up—and you have wrestled the gator into submission. This is where hot dogs like Williams and his crew begin their tricks, shoving their heads and hands into toothy mouths and bantering with the audience. The final—and most important—step is the dismount. Once you let the gator go, it is likely to be a little bit fussy about the person who has been pinning it down. Flip the gator, quickly, onto its back as you lift yourself off. Laid flat, belly up, it will fall into a temporary catatonic trance. And that's when you put some distance between yourself and the alligator, because that trance won't last for long.

THE SECRETS TO A GREAT (GUN) DOG

IF YOU WANT TO enjoy having a great gun dog in the field (and by the hearth), you've got to start with basic training, and most of that happens at home. For Mike Stewart, owner of Mississippi's legendary Wildrose Kennels, a list of rules for successfully training dogs, if he's allowed to elaborate, has been known to stretch into days on end, but here are his five proven ways to end up with a great pooch—and a dog that'll hunt.

1. BUILD TRUST: "No matter what day it is, no matter where you are in the world with your dog—doesn't matter if you're in New York City or on a farm in Mississippi—you have to be confident in your relationship with the dog. That takes time and work. It's about building trust between the two of you."

2. BE THE LEADER: "As either a trainer or a dog's master, you need to be calm, controlled, consistent, and confident at all times. It's all about pack mentality, and dogs won't follow an unstable dog—or an unstable leader. Eventually, they just won't do it."

3. MAKE HAY SLOWLY: "People rush too much in training their dogs. They want them to learn a specific habit or skill, and then they want to test them right away. They often take a dog into the field before it's ready. It takes longer to train a solid habit in a dog than you'd

think. I go by the five-times-five-times-two rule. The dog has to perform the same habit five times, in five different situations, and do it at least twice under those circumstances before you're getting anywhere close. In fact, doing five-times-five-times a few weeks, working with them every day, is even better. Then you know you might be near a behavior you can trust in the field."

4. WORK THEM AND PRAISE THEM: "A dog wants to please its master. And there's nothing wrong with praising it every time it does. The way I see it, most dogs are just out for a good time. I equate them with frat boys at Ole Miss. Yeah, it's fun to stand around with a plastic cup of beer and a cigarette. But if you show them there's value in work beyond that, if you stop that behavior and show them there's more that's

possible in their life? Motivate them to see other, bigger rewards? Well, both the frat boy and the dog might very well adopt the new behavior. Then you reinforce it, and that new behavior is still fun. It's just a different kind of fun."

5. GET THE RIGHT DOG: "If you're a young professional working long hours and living in a small apartment in a big city, even if your dad had German shorthaired pointers all the time when you grew up, that's still the wrong dog for your situation. Know who you are and what you want from a dog. Do breed research, then research inside that breed. Consult professionals. Different types of dogs have been developed for different things. Think about your life and what you want from your dog. That's fair to both of you."

A BASSMASTER'S SECRET WEAPON

THINK FLY FISHERMEN ARE finicky about their tackle? They've got nothing on the bass guys.

Just look at them. The average fly fisherman manages to fit everything he needs in a vest or one of those quaint little chest packs, whereas bass fishermen generally require a boatload of lures and at minimum a half dozen rods. There's a reason the tackle industry is worth around $6 billion a year.

But for all the spinnerbaits, buzzbaits, chatterbaits, jerkbaits, crankbaits, walking baits, and swim baits that have come since, there's still one simple rig that remains the do-it-all, no b.s., get me in the water and let me do my thing setup you can fish just about anywhere, anytime. And we have some savvy Southerners to thank for it.

It's called the Texas rig, and most accounts date its invention to the 1950s, shortly after the Creme Lure Company developed what is widely considered the first plastic worm. It wasn't long before the lure caught on big-time, and founder Nick Creme set up shop in Tyler, Texas. Although Creme's original design included hooks built into the worms, Lone Star anglers came up with their own way to fish these then-revolutionary baits, and the rig that will now forever be associated with the state has withstood the test of time for a reason. It's easy to use, versatile, and effective (and cheap). All you need is the proverbial hook, line, and sinker. And a plastic worm.

To rig it, slide a bullet-shaped weight onto the line with the thin side facing the rod and tie on a hook. Stick the point of the hook through the head of the worm about a quarter inch, then bring it out the belly side of the worm and slide the worm up the hook shank so the head rests against the hook's eye. Rotate the hook so that the point faces toward the belly and then bury the point back into the worm. This keeps it from snagging in weeds and cover, which is often where the fish are (as those Texas anglers knew well).

Cast it out, let it settle on the bottom, and then twitch it, hop it, or drag it back. There's not really a wrong way to fish it. Sometimes you might want to go slower, sometimes faster. Let the fish tell you. When you feel a thump, set the hook.

There are, naturally, some finer points. Nowadays fishermen often use an offset shank hook, which has a bend at the eye that helps the worm sit nice and flat.

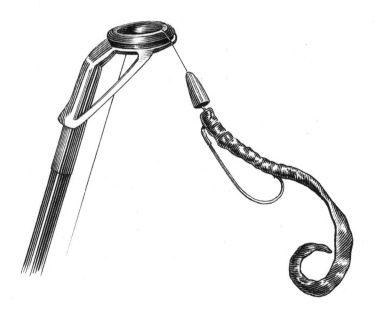

You can also rig it "Texposed" by pushing the point of the hook through the worm (or just barely underneath, called skin hooking). And when fishing heavier cover, anglers often "peg" the weight directly in front of the worm. The time-honored, and most likely Southern-devised, method for accomplishing this is to simply jam a toothpick through the narrow end of the weight and then break it off. The more modern, and most likely Northern-devised, method is to buy some specially made little rubber thingies to jam through the weight. But the basic rig really hasn't changed, or needed to, in a half century.

It probably goes without saying that there are now on the order of nine gazillion different kinds of plastic craws, creatures, lizards, bugs, and various other creepy crawlies to choose from. But for all of bass fishing's modern innovations ($6 billion, remember?), nothing has yet to supplant the good old Texas-rigged plastic worm. It just keeps catching fish.

CLOSE-QUARTER CASTS

ON THE WIDE-OPEN RIVERS out west, fly fishermen can throw a flamboyant cast without worrying too much about what's behind or above them. In the waters of the southern Appalachians, though—where fishermen are more likely to be picking through winding mountain streams, stumbling through brush, and wading in pools roofed by low-hanging branches—the typical cast can end up hooking more foliage than trout. That's where the roll cast comes into play. An understated but effective toss, it's the easiest way to land a fly in tight quarters without tangling your line.

To pull it off, raise your rod steadily to about the eleven o'clock position. Let the line and the fly drag across the water toward you as you pull the rod back. Do not, at any point, stop moving—the key to this cast is constant motion.

As you pull the line, it will begin to arc behind you in a D-shaped formation. Once you have raised the rod to the back-cast position, snap it forward quickly. The line should rise in a looping motion behind you and fall forward onto the water.

HANDLING SNAKES

FOR THE CENTURIES THAT Southerners have been living in close proximity to snakes, we have spun stories about how to treat a venomous bite. Some of us learned to suck out the poison, others to cut out the wound, others to tourniquet the affected limb.

All bunk, says Captain Jeff Fobb of Florida's Miami-Dade Fire Rescue, which boasts an entire unit, called Venom One, dedicated to treating snakebite victims. "The best thing you can do is get to a hospital." The only real way to treat the bite of a venomous snake is with the appropriate antivenin, and intensive medical care. Immediately following a bite, Fobb says, your focus should be on staying calm and stationary—avoiding, at

least, an increased heartbeat, which could move venom more quickly through your bloodstream—and calling in the professionals.

But lest you think there is nothing you can do, consider this: Fobb's surveys of snakebite victims show around 85 percent of them are *provoking* snakes when they are bitten. Authorities elsewhere report similar statistics. "Oftentimes, there are middle-aged guys and alcohol involved," says David Cooper, president of the North Carolina Herpetological Society.

Apart from not harassing the natives, a few other simple guidelines can keep you from having to deal with a snakebite in the first place. First, know when the snakes in your area are active. The cold-blooded reptiles generally come out of hiding in the warm-weather months. You'll often find them sunning them-selves in the early morning and hunting in the evening.

"Maintain situational awareness," Fobb says. "Do not put your hands where you can't see them." Likewise, do not walk through tall grass with-out sturdy boots on unless you shuffle a stick ahead of your feet. Do not send your children out to play in a yard that has not been mowed in a few weeks. If you see your dog playing with a snake, grab the dog while remaining as far away from the snake as possible. Like most animals, snakes are more interested in getting out of the way than sticking around to cause trouble. Respect them and they are likely to respect you. But just in case—keep the address of the nearest hospital handy.

SOUTHERN SPORTING DOGS

THROUGH LONG JAUNTS IN the field and quiet nights by the fire, canine companions have been close at Southerners' heels since well before the days of George Washington—a passionate foxhound breeder who, at the height of the Revolutionary War, famously insisted upon returning a British general's captured terrier to its owner. Apart from the imports, though, over the years a handful of distinct breeds were developed specifically for use below the Mason-Dixon Line. These sporting dogs come with long pedigrees and years of service in Southern fields, swamps, and bays—and, most important, the home.

BOYKIN SPANIEL

Legend has it that the ur-Boykin was a stray spaniel that followed a Spartanburg, South Carolina, banker home from church sometime in the early 1900s. Given to Whit Boykin, a local planter and sportsman, the little stray proved to be such a fine hunting companion that Boykin made it the basis for a breed. Competent in field, in blind, and in boat (where its diminutive size gives it an advantage over larger hunting dogs), the Boykin spaniel is known for its friendly temperament, loyalty, and near-inexhaustible energy—whether flushing, retrieving, or running circles around the family living room.

CATAHOULA LEOPARD DOG

The history of the Catahoula Leopard Dog is as crowded and long as that of its home state, Louisiana. The breed is believed to descend from three distinct sources: the dogs kept by native Choctaws, the stocky Spanish canines introduced by sixteenth-century conquistador Hernando de Soto, and the late-arriving French Beauceron. Early settlers in Louisiana put the Catahoula to work on farms, where its herding instincts and protective nature made it a natural for watching over livestock. An excellent tracker and highly intelligent, it's also been known to scramble up a tree in pursuit of small game, and it's been used for centuries to hunt wild boar.

CHESAPEAKE BAY RETRIEVER

The Chesapeake Bay retriever was bred sometime in the nineteenth century to retrieve birds for the duck hunters of the Mid-Atlantic. A water-loving canine with a courageous spirit—necessary for hunting over cold and sometimes rough waters—the breed is notoriously stubborn. But a steady, confident trainer can harness the dog's natural work ethic to mold a puppy into a faithful duck-hunting partner as well as a fun-loving family companion.

PLOTT HOUND

Johannes Plott arrived in the United States in the mid-eighteenth century with a fleet of hunting dogs from his native Germany. Although he insisted upon keeping the line pure, his descendants in the mountains of North Carolina crossed the German hounds with local breeds to develop the hunting dog known today as the Plott Hound. Bred to hunt large game, the Plott is a tough customer that is absolutely fearless in the field. Sounding its loud, high-pitched bawl, it will navigate deep water, steep slopes, and thick brush in any number of adverse conditions without losing focus on its quarry.

BLUE LACY

In 1858, the Lacy brothers migrated from Kentucky to the Texas Hill Country, where the hog farmers bred a new kind of ranch dog from a handful of local breeds—the greyhound, scent hound, and coyote thought to be among them. The Blue Lacy was a common sight in rural Texas until the mid-twentieth century, when the decline of the family ranch decreased demand for working dogs. But today, the breed is experiencing a renaissance fueled in part by hunters who have discovered its talents in the field. With a powerful nose and high trainability, the Blue Lacy is well suited to tracking, treeing, and any other activity that requires athleticism and endurance.

CATCH AND PICK A BLUE CRAB

GENERATIONS OF Southerners have passed long, lazy days of summer catching blue crabs. Among them is Lee Barber, game manager at Sea Island's Broadfield sporting club in Georgia. "To me," he says, "there is no better way to spend an afternoon than going out to catch crabs and then sitting down to cook, pick, and eat them."

The catching part is easy. A simple piece of string tied to a chicken neck and a weight (just about anything from a large bolt to a small lead weight will work) is a proven method. Toss the chicken neck in and wait until you see your line moving ever so slightly. This is the crab. It's scurrying on the bottom with this magnificent find clamped tightly in its claws, and it has no intention of letting go. Use this last point to your advantage. Gently start pulling in the line until you can just see the crab beneath the surface. Then slip a dip net under it, and deposit it in a bucket. This is crabbing. You can use a hoop net or even an honest-to-goodness crab trap, but what fun is that? After all, it's human versus crab for God's sake.

When you are ready to cook, flush your bucket of crabs with water until the water runs clean. Discard any dead crabs unless you have kept them on ice, and drop the rest into a large pot of salted water. Some cooks like to add Old Bay or other seasonings for extra flavor. If you use it, don't be shy. Boil for ten to fifteen minutes. (Of course, if you're in the vicinity of the Chesapeake, you'll be steaming your crabs. No need to send letters. We know this.) Then dump them, drain them, let them cool a little bit, and get to picking. The good Mr. Barber has some thoughts on this.

1. FLIP the crab over. Twist off the legs and remove the claws. It's perfectly acceptable to put the meaty end of the leg in your mouth and with a satisfied puckering sound inhale the thin strands of meat.

2. CRACK the claws with a mallet or the handle of a butter knife, taking care not to crush them, and pull them apart to get to the meat inside.

3. USE the sharp tip of a claw to pry the "apron" off the crab's underside. Then use your thumbs to pull off the top shell.

4. SCRAPE the crab's yellow insides out with a finger. (Seasoned crabbers call the stuff "mustard" and consider it a delicacy. It is safe to consume in nonpolluted areas. But don't feel guilty about passing it up.) Then pop off and discard the gray gills—known as dead man's fingers—that sit on top of the meat.

5. PLACE your thumbs firmly on the two sides of the crab and snap it in half. Then snap those halves in half. Use your fingers or a small cocktail fork to pick the flaky white meat from the crevices in the shell.

6. REPEAT.

HOW TO TALK TO A GAME WARDEN

BEN MOÏSE WAS a game warden around Charleston, South Carolina, for twenty-four years. Over the course of his quarter century in the field, he dealt with ne'er-do-wells of all stripes—trigger-happy hunters, slippery fishermen, even drug runners. "Those of us that have been in the business long enough have seen it all," he says. "And we have highly developed fertilizer detectors." While we trust that you will never need to hoodwink a game warden, here are a few things Moïse advises you to keep in mind should your trigger finger slip a few minutes before sunrise or if you honestly lose count and end up with one fish too many in your cooler.

BE RESPECTFUL: "The last thing written on a ticket is the amount of the fine, and that can range from the minimum, which is not so bad, to a catastrophe. I've run into a few hunters who considered themselves genealogists and misquoted my ancestry from two monkeys on the other side of Adam and Eve. They got the absolute maximum, and I was searching for a way to write them a second ticket. Most of the time, game wardens are not looking to be unnecessarily burdensome. But if people keep talking, they might keep checking and find things that they could have ignored or overlooked. I'm not saying it's a vengeful thing. It's just a natural reaction."

SHUT UP: "Never say more than you need to. Answer questions directly and don't incriminate yourself. Once, I caught a fellow shooting waterfowl seven or eight minutes early. He said he'd heard other people up and down the river shooting. And he was right—that river was full of violators. Then he said, 'What makes your watch so much more accurate than mine?' I said, 'Let me see your watch,' and he admitted that he didn't have one. I only gave him a warning, but I considered that very weaselly."

BE PREPARED: "One should have the required license. If you don't—whether you didn't buy one or just don't have it on you—then believe me, your excuse won't work. We've heard it. The dog ate your license, or it blew out the window, or it went through the washing machine. You can tell it to the judge."

RULES OF THE ROAD TRIP

BY DANIEL WALLACE

THEY USED TO BE called *grand tours*. Monocled men in bowler hats (tea-drinking birders, pinkies extended) called it *motoring*. The first recorded road trips were taken in chariots, in Egypt, more than three thousand years ago; the most recent on record as of this writing was by Mark L. and Sylvia J., of Atlanta. They took I-20 West out of the city and then hit I-65 South in Birmingham (stopping, briefly, to say hello to some of Mark's cousins) and after about two hundred miles disappeared somewhere near Exit 37, about thirty minutes from their destination, Gulf Shores. Four happy hours later, they arrived.

What happened between that exit and Gulf Shores? No one knows but Mark and Sylvia, and it came as a surprise even to them. That's the heart of the road trip, its epistemological center: not knowing what comes next. The explorers who came before us had to clear away a lot of brush and scare away a lot of bears before they could see where they were going. Our challenge, in this world of scrupulously detailed maps and satellite-guided tours, is to reclaim that same spirit of adventure. Here are some guidelines to seeing what they saw: nothing—and everything.

1. ROAD TRIPS ARE NOT VACATIONS: Vacations are planned months in advance; they are researched, tested by focus groups, contrasted with vacations past via PowerPoint in an effort to maximize the chances of creating new,

vibrant, photographable memories. On a vacation you stay in chain hotels with room service and indoor pools. You make sure you bring a lot of sunblock. You get someone to house-sit and walk the dog and water the garden. On road trips you stay at motels called the Peach Blossom, where there's no elevator because there's no second floor, where the 1950s-era illuminated vacancy sign advertises free air-conditioning and ice, where wireless means that the lamps don't work. You sneak the dog in, but they don't care, not really. Everyone you meet on a road trip loves dogs.

2. GET LOST: A road trip wherein one does not get lost is not a road trip; it's something else, the same way Pringles aren't really potato chips. If you don't get lost, you'll miss all the best yard art, the secret quarries, all the little timeless towns secreted away on the other side of that mysterious hill. And three-legged dogs—you'll miss them, too.

I once got lost in South Carolina and got the idea for my third book. I passed a sign that read WELCOME TO THE STRAWBERRY CAPITAL OF THE WORLD! Sign said it was right around the bend, and I could not wait. What a magical place I was about to enter! A spotless, happy town full of handsome men and beautiful women, with a median age of thirty-two, all giving away bright red, luscious strawberries, strawberries as big as cats, dripping juice. The difference between what I imagined and the reality of what I found—an abandoned Main Street, dark empty buildings, tire fires, and lots of three-legged dogs—is what led me to write *The Watermelon King*. True story.

3. GET OFF THE HIGHWAY: Highways were built by people who want you to get somewhere, not go somewhere. Better to take a road. The best are well-tended paths, paved as if in afterthought, circuitously cutting through ancient forests and someone's backyard.

There are risks, yes. Once you get off the interstate, your trip is at the whim of every farmer with a thousand-year-old tractor who picks the exact wrong moment to pull in front of your four-wheel funmobile. He's driving to work, maybe to plow or . . . whatever it is tractors do. But on a two-lane blacktop as thin as a piece of string, you can't pass him without risking your life, and now you won't get to Loxahatchee before nightfall. You kind of wanted to watch the sunset in Loxahatchee. But think about this: There is no roadside on a highway, and therefore there are no roadside landmarks. Roadside landmarks peculiar to the South: mermaids, alligators, jewel-encrusted caverns, pecan stands, fruit purveyors in derelict lean-tos, shaded beneath a rusting corrugated-metal roof that appears to have been salvaged from some local Armageddon, practically giving away the best apples you've ever had in your life. And boiled-peanut stands. An admission (and for a Southerner it's a big, brave one): I've never stopped at a boiled-peanut stand; I'd sooner stop at a roadside sushi stand. And let's call it what it is: a soggy peanut. You call it boiled because no one's going to stop at a soggy-peanut stand.

4. PLAY GAMES: Sad how the automobile has gone from being a playground to a prison. When I was a kid, I rolled around in the way-back like a basketball, wrestling with my little sister or pleading with the passing truckers to please, please blow their horns, with the traditional downward thrust of the arm, hand fisted, miming as though they might actually be pulling a rope. How irritating that must have been for them: child after child begging for the same noise. But there is no "way-back" for the kids these days. They're strapped in like Hannibal Lecter. A family road trip is too often a military exercise in quiet subordination. Does anyone even moon anymore? One can't help but get nostalgic about the preteen moon.

Still, there are some acceptable games left to play. Everybody knows them: I Spy, 20 Questions, License Plate, Slug-a-Bug, Name That Tune. Hold Your Breath When You're in a Tunnel/Passing a Graveyard/ When Your Father Passes Gas. But my favorite is simply called Roadkill. There is no game more Southern than this one, and it's fun, especially if you're driving through Mississippi. Count the dead possums, armadillos, deer, raccoons, birds, snakes, and frogs, whether they're smashed flat on the faded white lane-dividing line or unceremoniously shoved to the shoulder. The first to a hundred wins.

5. GO ALONG FOR THE RIDE: There's an art to everything these days, people say, from the forced poeticism of YouTube videos to shooting skeet and noodling. But road-tripping is an art. It's not unlike writing a novel: the writer (rider?) tells herself she knows where she's going, but she doesn't really know. There's an imaginary destination, a sparkling mirage on the horizon, but all it provides is a general direction. As she writes, the story opens up to her the same way the world does when she turns left instead of right, stops here instead of there. The road she ends up taking is as much a surprise to her as it is to us. Barreling down the two-lane blacktop with the wind in her hair and time on her hands is a mystical splendor unmatched, unmatchable. She may never get where she thinks she's going, but that's okay. Soon—tomorrow, the next day, next week, or next year—she can just turn around if she wants to. Because while there's nothing better than leaving home, there's nothing better than coming back.

Part Five

HOME & GARDEN

IN PRAISE OF THE SOUTHERN GARDEN

BY ROBERT HICKS

F A GARDEN SERVED AS THE CRADLE OF HUMANITY, THEN IT'S SAFE TO SAY THAT SOUTHERNERS HAVE NEVER FORGOTTEN THAT SUCH A PLACE IS HALLOWED GROUND. FROM THE VERY EARLIEST ACCOUNTS OF IMMIGRATION, IN THE SEVENTEENTH CENTURY, MOVING THROUGH THE EIGHTEENTH AND NINETEENTH CENTURIES, GARDENS WERE AT THE CENTER OF LIFE IN THE SOUTH. SOME MIGHT EXPLAIN THIS AS THE SIMPLE NECESSITY TO SURVIVE, BUT FROM THE VERY BEGINNING, THE SOUTHERNER'S PASSION FOR THE GARDEN REACHED FAR BEYOND BASE SURVIVAL.

Southern gardens have come down through the ages in all shapes and sizes, with myriad plant life, ranging from the most common of vegetables and herbs to the rarest of ornamentals and fruit trees. Our love of growing things has stood the test of both time and generations, whether it's a bean patch mixed with hollyhocks, daylilies, narcissus, and an old rose outside the door of a log cabin; the gardens of the great town houses in Charleston, Savannah, Richmond, and Nashville; the

Creole potager gardens along the River Road of Louisiana; or a grand plantation's formal gardens, with elaborate geometric beds lined with clipped boxwood hedges.

In June 1851, noted Southern clergyman and planter Charles Colcock Jones returned to Maybank, his family's Sea Island plantation at the mouth of Georgia's Medway River. He soon wrote his wife, Mary, who was staying in New England. It's very telling that it was with news of the gardens that he expressed his love to her. He wrote, "Everything just as you left it, and all reminding me of my love, my sweet Mary. If I look out on the flowers and smell their fragrance, she planted and trained them with her own hands; if I look at the trees and the garden with its fruits, its oranges and figs and pomegranates, its pears and peaches and plums and apples, they were all set out under her eye and pruned and fostered by her care."

Throughout the nineteenth century, visitors from other parts of the country and Europe were awed by the South's gardens, filling travel books and diaries with descriptions of our labor and the fruit of it. There are our more famous presidential practitioners, including Jefferson, Washington, and Jackson's wife, Rachel, but the truth is that most everyone—rich or poor—was a gardener. Plants and seeds were passed along from neighbor to neighbor or ordered from garden catalogues, probably in more abundance than they are today, despite the significant growth in population. Sadly enough, whether speaking of tomatoes or pears, apples or figs, we now have only a fraction of what could have been found in most plots 150 years ago.

What has often been called the Golden Age of Gardens was born in Europe and America on the heels of the Civil War. Though much of the South struggled during Reconstruction, gardens still thrived across the region. New ones were born, often grander than anything we'd ever known before. Rose beds had never been more spectacular; boxwoods had never been bigger. From Virginia and Maryland and all the way to the new subtropical gardens of South Florida, the South blossomed during this time, but many of its greatest gardens would fall to the one-two punch of the Great Depression and the Second World War.

With modernity and suburban sprawl, it's easy for us to forget or ignore the great regard that generations of Southerners have had for raising up plants for business and pleasure. Thankfully, Southerners have begun to rediscover what's been lost. We may never reach the same heights again, but it seems likely that with this latest garden renaissance and renewed interest in heirlooms, the saving and trading of seeds, and all the rest, we'll enter a Silver Age of Gardens. We may never recover anything close to the selection of the past, but with the combined efforts of passionate gardeners, historians, and nurseries, many plants once considered lost have been rediscovered. The South is ripe for this renaissance.

The scarlet thread that runs through at least four hundred years of gardening in this botanically and culturally rich region is our endless interest in the soil beneath our feet—not only for the sustenance it gives but also for the beauty it slowly reveals from within. From humble dirt, helped along by an abundance of rain and sunshine, heaven indeed comes to earth, and working in the midst of all that is truly one of our most essential human experiences. Forget your green thumbs; cultivate a green soul.

SHADES OF THE SOUTH

PROXIMITY TO THE EQUATOR determines lots of things: quality of the light, fertility of the soil, temperature, and even the choice of paint colors. In the South, you'll find distinct hues influenced by both geography and history. They also fluctuate—much like the light—from electric and bright to moody and morose. And naturally, they all come with good stories.

1. CHARLESTON GREEN: Legend has it that ever-stylish Charlestonians were disappointed with the lackluster buckets of black paint the government sent down for use during Reconstruction. They did their best to give it some panache by mixing in yellow and green, creating a lagoon-like hue that's still a signature of the Holy City. The color is most popular on shutters, trim work, and wrought iron—or on a rocking chair out on the front porch.

2. HAINT BLUE: According to Gullah lore, haints—a vicious clan of ghosts floating between the worlds of the living and the dead—were said to be unable to cross over water. Which is why you'll see front doors, porch ceilings, and exterior trim work painted in this lovely shade of light blue. Some say it keeps flies away, too.

3. CREOLE PINK: Maybe it was inspired by the Caribbean sunset—or the sand.

Or maybe it's just that it does a great job reflecting the worst of the summer heat. Whatever the origin, you'll find this soft pink used especially in coastal towns such as New Orleans and Savannah.

4. MONTICELLO YELLOW: It should come as no surprise that a man of such voracious intellectual appetites as Thomas Jefferson would choose a color so bright and bold. This deep, warm yellow was resurrected in the dining room of the third president's Virginia mansion in 2010, after researchers found proof of its presence in the home during Jefferson's later years.

5. HEMINGWAY GREEN: Inspired by the glint of light on the edge of a palm frond, Ernest Hemingway's second wife, Pauline, a former editor at *Vogue*, chose this sun-splashed green—closest in hue to the inside of an avocado—for the shutters of the author's Key West villa.

RAISING YARDBIRDS

SOUTHERNERS HAVE BEEN waking up and living with chickens since the first New World settlements were established. But sometime during the last century, as eggs appeared in neat rows and breasts came wrapped in cellophane, we forgot how much our forebears enjoyed having some yardbirds around.

Chickens are an easy-to-keep and plentiful source of food and fertilizer. They also snatch mosquitoes and no-see-ums on the wing. Left to follow their whims in a good yard, they're fascinating to watch. Fortunately for the biddies, scores of Southerners both rural and urban are rediscovering all this. Still, chickens aren't for everyone. For the curious, we got the scoop on coops and poop from ninth-generation South Carolina farmer Helen Legare-Floyd.

WHAT WILL THE NEIGHBORS THINK?

Some cities and neighborhoods don't allow chickens. But if yours does, you might have to forgo the ladies' having a man around. "The two best ways to keep the neighbors from complaining," Legare-Floyd says, "are to avoid roosters—and to give them plenty of eggs." Hens make a little noise while laying, but they're generally docile compared with the loudmouthed males. And you can consider sharing some backyard-fresh eggs now and then a little neighborly payoff.

HOW MUCH WORK IS INVOLVED?

While a flock of chickens won't be as in-your-face needy as, say, a new puppy, you have to keep an eye on the birds. "You can put a big feeder and waterer out so you won't have to feed and water them every day," Legare-Floyd says, "but you'll still have to look in on them." Expect to collect eggs, check food and water levels, and peek in the coop daily.

HOW DO YOU KEEP THEM SAFE?

"People don't think about what a predator problem we have down here," Legare-Floyd says. Dogs, foxes, raccoons, hawks—they're all out there, and they're all out to get your poultry. A secure coop is an important investment, and you'll need to keep it well maintained and protected. If you live somewhere that tolerates roosters, they can help deter some of the more common predators.

HOW MUCH SPACE DO THEY NEED?

One thing you never want to do to your chickens is crowd them. "Chickens tend to get upset real easily," Legare-Floyd says, "and when they do—when they're crowded or unhappy—they won't lay, and they tend to peck on each other." Claustrophobic conditions can prompt chickens to peck each other to death. For happy birds, allow about four square feet in the coop for each full-grown chicken (more if they're cooped up full-time).

WHAT ABOUT THE LAWN?

Chickens are going to scratch, so you can surrender a corner of your yard or invest in a mobile coop. A coop on wheels keeps the flock from wearing out one spot, plus it helps spread natural fertilizer all around. "Chickens are just pooping *machines*," Legare-Floyd says. "And the grass is always greener where they've been. Their poop is amazing fertilizer."

A TASTE FOR HEIRLOOMS

BACK IN 1980, a neighbor of North Carolinian Gordon Schronce gave him a few peanuts. They looked normal enough from the outside, but when Schronce cracked them open, he discovered the legumes were sheathed in distinctive black skins rather than the more common red. Intrigued, he saved the peanuts (a.k.a. seeds) to replant and harvest the following season. Year after year, he saved the largest, blackest ones and replanted. Fast-forward a few decades and Schronce's carefully cultivated strain of black peanut, the Schronce's Deep Black, was introduced to the gardening world, to the delight of many a goober lover. (If you count yourself as one, try them fried in canola oil—alongside some red-skinned peanuts—and sprinkled with sea salt.)

The same sort of story repeats itself across the Southern plant kingdom: Find seed, grow seed, save seed, and pass it along, so the rest of us can enjoy its fruits. And enjoy them we do. Heirlooms—which are open-pollinated, as opposed to hybrids—haven't been this popular for generations.

Like the word *antique*, though, *heirloom* can describe varieties of plants in a wide range of ages. Some might deem it appropriate to include anything older than fifty years; others take a more conservative approach, limiting it to any variety dating to 1940 or earlier. "Back before World War II, produce was still locally grown and people were saving seeds on their own," says Ira Wallace, of Virginia-based Southern Exposure Seed

Exchange, which offers Schronce's Deep Black and hundreds of other heirlooms in its seed catalogue.

What makes these older varieties so special—that is, why do folks drool over them, despite their sometimes unfamiliar, even strange, appearances? For one thing, they taste better. After all, you won't catch a gardener saving the seeds of anything that doesn't measure up. At the opposite end of the spectrum, large-scale chemical agriculture runs breeding programs that create and select varieties based on their ability to be grown in Anywhere, USA, consistently produce fruit of a uniform appearance, and withstand being shipped long distances.

Flavor, to put it mildly, isn't a huge consideration.

Big Ag also breeds for disease resistance. But heirlooms are often naturally drought and pest resistant, having adapted to regional conditions the old-fashioned way. This is precisely why finding an heirloom seed that is native to your area will make growing it all the more rewarding.

But the best part about growing heirloom varieties in your backyard is that you get to eat an original foodstuff—with unique flavors, colors, and shapes—that you simply will not find at the supermarket. Every bite seems brighter, more intense. And every seed, just like Schronce's Deep Black peanut, has a story to tell.

THE PERFECT TOMATO

OF ALL THE SOUTHERN heirlooms, none is more beloved than the tomato. Stacked between two slices of bread slathered in Duke's mayonnaise or sliced and sprinkled with salt and pepper, a perfectly ripe heirloom tomato is transformative, forever ruining your ability to enjoy modern hybrids; you'll always taste what's not there. These days, heirloom orbs in pink, yellow, purple, and orange can be found in gardens across the South, due in large part to the efforts of organizations such as the Seed Savers Exchange. North Carolina green thumb Craig LeHoullier joined Seed Savers in 1986, and after nurturing more than a thousand different tomato varieties over nearly thirty seasons, he's *the* 'mater guru down South. With a little help from LeHoullier, you don't have to be a pro to have a bumper crop hanging from the vines come summer.

"Tomatoes are not difficult to grow," LeHoullier says. But that doesn't mean you can plunk a seed in the ground and send up a prayer. Heirloom varieties in particular are often indeterminate, meaning, if left unchecked, vines can easily reach heights of eight feet or more. Staking or caging will keep them from taking over your plot. Full sun and well-drained soil are the basic conditions that must be met for your tomato plants to succeed. "But adequate watering is critical," LeHoullier says, "especially during our very hot Southern summers."

The time to plant is determined by weather, so you'll want to check with a garden expert in your area, but generally tomatoes are planted in the early spring and ready by mid- to late summer. Retaining some green around the shoulders is a common genetic trait among heirloom varieties, but if you do pick too soon, simply set them out on the kitchen counter to finish ripening. And never put them in the fridge, which will sap flavor. Besides, once the neighbors get wind of your bounty, chances are you won't have many extras.

CRAIG LeHOULLIER'S TOP FIVE HEIRLOOM TOMATOES

1. NEPAL (medium; scarlet): "This is the variety that converted me from hybrid to heirloom tomato grower," LeHoullier says. Forgiving of extreme heat, it grows well in the Deep South, and its smooth, round fruit packs an intense sweet flavor that will likely convert you too.

2. CHEROKEE PURPLE (large; dusky rose, nearly purple): Cultivated by Cherokee Indians in Tennessee for hundreds of years, this large beefsteak tomato is resilient and considered one of the best tasting heirlooms, prized for its complex sweet flavors. It makes a killer tomato sandwich.

3. LILLIAN'S YELLOW HEIRLOOM (large; very pale yellow to orange): Visually stunning with the flavor to match, this mildly sweet citrusy tomato is a juicy late-summer treat. But if temperatures in your area regularly reach (and stay) above 90 degrees, try one of the more robust medium-size heirlooms.

4. BRANDYWINE (very large; pink): A cult favorite among growers and chefs, the Brandywine dates back more than one hundred years and is favored for its exceptionally rich flavor. But like Lillian's Yellow, it doesn't produce well when exposed to intense heat for extended periods.

5. ANNA RUSSIAN (medium; heart shaped; pink): This hardy oxheart tomato will flourish in most weather conditions. Brought to America by a Russian immigrant, it has a full old-fashioned flavor and is known for being particularly juicy.

THE FIVE-MINUTE GUIDE TO COLLECTING

IN A REGION so tied to our country's early history, it's perhaps not surprising that Southerners have developed a particular penchant for collecting old things—antiques and objects that speak to both the land and the culture. The best collections require a passion that goes beyond mere financial investment (though a well-curated assemblage can be that too), and amassing one can, of course, take a lifetime. But if you've got a touch of the bug yourself, here's a brief primer on some of the South's most popular and approachable collectibles.

OYSTER PLATES: In the Victorian era, when eating oysters was newly in vogue, hostesses in the United States and Europe served them up not on the half shell over ice but on decorative, specially designed oyster plates. Production slowed almost to a halt after World War I, as years of overfarming hurt the oyster industry and the formality of Victorian life fell by the

wayside. But you can still find vintage oyster plates in antique shops and collectors' cabinets all over the South. The most valuable plates are hand painted—some with floral designs, others with sea creatures or images of oysters themselves—and sell for thousands of dollars.

To start your collection, say Steve Bonner and his wife, Lynn, owners of Kilmarnock Antique Gallery in Virginia, seek out originals from coveted manufacturers like Haviland and Union Porcelain Works. (You will find those companies' marks—HC and UPW, respectively—on the bottoms of their plates.) Most important, once you have a few oyster plates to your name, avoid either hanging them up or eating on them, both of which can cause significant damage.

JULEP CUPS: The silver tumbler known as the julep cup has a long history as the Southerner's preferred vessel for an icy summertime cocktail. Though commonly associated with Kentucky—famous Bluegrass State silversmiths include Asa Blanchard and William Kendrick—julep cups have been produced all over the South going back more than two centuries. "In terms of their association with racing and the outdoors, drinking out of silver was an immediate way to communicate wealth and status," says Daniel Ackermann, associate curator of the Museum of Early Southern Decorative Arts in Winston-Salem, North Carolina. "But you could also carry the cups in a bag and they wouldn't break." Today, antique tumblers can fetch between several hundred dollars and several thousand dollars.

The value of a julep cup depends on a few things. First, the material: Julep cups are commonly made of coin silver, sterling silver, silver plate, or pewter. Though coin silver, produced in the nineteenth century from European silver coins, is not the purest of the four, it is popular with collectors. Sterling silver is close to pure silver, while cups stamped "silver plate" are only silver coated, and pewter is a tin-based alloy.

A julep cup's maker can be as important as its substance. The marks of some prominent silversmiths command high prices, such as the highly collectible Presidential series cups from Wakefield-Scearce, stamped on the bottom with an eagle and the current president's initials. But while a silversmith's stamp can send a cup's value through the stratosphere, a prominent monogram can pull it right back down to earth. If a cup is monogrammed, its value will most likely decrease—that is, except in the rare case that the initials bear some historical significance.

DECOYS: Though originally crafted as utilitarian hunting aids, well-made waterfowl decoys now sell for thousands—even hundreds of thousands—of dollars to enthusiastic collectors all over the country. Even decorative decoys display telltale signs of their origins. Decoys from the upper Chesapeake Bay tend to be round bottomed and able to right themselves in rough water, while decoys from the calmer lower part of the bay sit on wide, flat bases. Carvers near the swifter Delaware River turn out hollow, lightweight birds, while decoys from North Carolina's Outer Banks, where wood was harder to come by, are traditionally made from canvas.

One of the most fascinating things about decoy collecting, says C. John Sullivan, Jr., a lifelong decoy enthusiast and the former director of the Havre de Grace Decoy Museum in Maryland, is that while there are plenty of big names in the field, it's not unheard of for a collector to come across an incredible piece shaped by an unknown hand—or for that piece to sell for big money.

ANTIQUE LINENS: "First and foremost, linens serve a practical purpose," says Jane Scott Hodges, founder of Louisiana-based Leontine Linens. "But from the beginning we have embellished them. Whether it was dying, quilting, printing, or appliqué, even the very earliest linens had aesthetic elements." It's becoming increasingly rare to find truly handmade modern examples, which is why vintage and antique linens—where beautiful handwork was the norm—remain so prized.

Cocktail napkins and handkerchiefs are some of the more common finds and generally sport price tags that are reasonable for the beginning collector. Antique linens are costly to mend, though, so check the edges, which will display the first signs of wear and tear. And be sure to review any purchase for stains; it's safe to say that an antique stain is a permanent one. That being said, with proper care these pieces will survive for a very long time—so your grandchildren might one day enjoy showing off your collection.

MEMORIES OF A SOUTHERN HOME

BY DOMINIQUE BROWNING

IF YOU HAD ASKED me, when I was a very little girl, what my father did, I would have told you he was a shooter. He shot guns. As far as I was then concerned, that was by far the most impressive thing about him. When I was a bit older, I understood that he was a doctor; a few years later, it occurred to me to wonder why a person whose livelihood was putting things right would want to blast things apart. Not a terribly original thought in the seventies, as everyone my age was protesting guns and wars and wearing headbands across their foreheads. Anyway, my father's guns have a great deal to do with my idea of Southern homes, as the first thing I heard about his Kentucky childhood was that he could lean out his window and shoot squirrels. As I said, this was impressive stuff: I was growing up in Connecticut, but it might as well have been Mars. My mother had grown up in Casablanca, Morocco, and was making sure we had a proper French upbringing. We certainly weren't allowed to play with guns.

Home, for my father, was a small town in western Kentucky called Hopkinsville. It took only one visit for me to fall in love with my grandparents' house. I learned to fish, and saw my first cow, in Kentucky. I used to pine for the house after we left, count the months until our return, and roam through the rooms in my daydreams. It was the house I longed to run away to whenever I got mad at my mother, my sisters, my piano teachers, my life. I wish I'd had the courage to go. Still, my father's Kentucky home long ago came to represent everything I love (and believe in) about Southern homes—and I've spent countless days and nights in homes in New Orleans and Texas.

I should say, my father's Kentucky *homes*. His parents had a small farmhouse on the outskirts of town, as well as the house in town, but the two have blended together in my recollection. It doesn't matter; they shared characteristics I've come to think of as classically Southern. They welcomed the out-of-doors; tree branches brushed windows (those poor squirrels!). The windows and doors were always screened and open, on the chance of catching a breeze, and the halls were designed to let air flow through; the architectural solutions for what we would now, in our climate-controlled days, call a green life had already been developed. The openness of the house in town also had to do with the people constantly going in and out—friends, relatives, neighbors; there seemed to be a busy, social quality to life in that house. Everyone was Sugar or Darlin' or Honey or, my favorite, Dear Heart. There was always someone rocking on a deep porch, and wide hallways gave on to staircases that led to upper floors—that, too, was alien

to me, and mysterious; we had always lived in one-story apartments and houses. The house was old and held a family's history in its rooms, which also, to my young mind, seemed key to a Southern home; Northern homes were new, and you had to invent a story for them.

The house neatly divided into rooms that were for work (cooking, sewing) and rooms in which one had to maintain proper decorum and sit primly, with hands folded, on horsehair sofas. I was allowed to take my books into the parlor and felt quite privileged about it. One day, when I was about five, I offered to read a story to my cousin, who was ten years older. She sat and listened quietly while I chatted and turned pages—and it wasn't until thirty years later that she confessed she hadn't been able to understand a word I was saying most of the time, as I had made up some language that mixed French and English—with a Northern accent, to make things worse. How gentle and polite she had been, how courteous; everyone was. The air of sweet graciousness that imbued every room in that house was something else that I came to associate with a Southern home, a quality of warm, reliable hospitality and pleasant manners. None of my feeling for what makes a Southern house has much to do with architectural expression or curtains or rugs or furniture—none of which I can remember, except for a certain darkness of wood. It's a spirit I recall so tenderly, a permeating system of values.

Food played an enormous role in our visits to Kentucky. I especially remember formal Sunday dinners (at lunchtime), for which everyone gathered around a large table. This, of course, meant that the house always smelled wonderful, for there was always something in the oven, usually something sweet. We said grace before meals and said prayers before bed; it was assumed that these rituals had become ours in our Connecticut home, which they hadn't. My mother complained during our visits about never understanding a word anyone was saying—the Southern accent was too much for her, and the same went for the Southern fare. It was all—the people and the food—too sweet. I have a photograph from the mid-fifties of her at a Kentucky picnic, standing in front of her pale, blond, ample, lantern-jawed mother-in-law. My mother is wearing a sophisticated, fitted strapless dress that flares out at the waist. Her waist is so tiny my father can fit his hands around it. She is in high heels—and wearing lipstick, as always—and with her dark wavy hair and large green eyes and olive skin, she looks like Sophia Loren come to the hoedown.

When the heat was unbearable, my sister and I were allowed to share a bed on the sleeping porch—an enchanting space that should definitely come back in style—but the bed was large and so tall we needed help getting into it. One night, I fell out and, frightened in the dark, wandered into the house, walking right through a large pan of chocolate cake that had been left to cool on the porch. There was a great fuss, I recall, with concern for my happiness, and much laughter about the cake squished between my toes. What a nice place, I remember thinking then. The next morning my grandmother had me lie down on a brown paper bag that had been cut open so that she could make a pattern of my body for a new dress—the house had a sewing room, which had the serene beauty of the purposeful. A gold light filtered past thin white curtains in the afternoon, my grandmother's head was bent quietly over her work, and I pawed through boxes of scraps to pick favorite prints for a quilt. Something was always being made. Everything was used; nothing was wasted.

When my oldest son was born, my parents came down to Texas to see us in the hospital. My father arrived beaming with pride, joy, and a great deal of excitement about the birth gift he had somehow managed to get past the security guards, but this being Texas, perhaps it hadn't been so hard. He presented his first grandson—who was a bit distracted by his own momentous discovery of my breast—with a beautiful little gun, a 20-gauge over-and-under Winchester, its receiver engraved with a delicate pattern. These days, my sons—and all their cousins—like nothing better than to hang out at Poppy's house, shooting at tin cans bobbing on the pond out back. The gun stays there. For the few hours during those visits, we're all back at the house of my dreams in Kentucky, basking in the grace of love handed down through the generations.

THE YEAR-ROUND CUTTING GARDEN

THE BEAUTY OF a well-planted flower garden doesn't end at the front door. "Southerners take such pride in their homes," says Charlotte, North Carolina–based landscape designer Laurie Durden, whose grandmother would head to the North Carolina mountains every Monday to cut fresh flowers for the house. "And the garden isn't separate from the home—it's part of the home. You want to bring it inside and share it with your family and guests."

Rather than cultivating a specific cutting garden (it can look too messy when flowers die or are cut if they're all in one place, she says), Durden recommends spreading unfussy, low-maintenance plants that produce beautiful blooms throughout your yard or garden. Her Southern-inspired season-by-season picks will have you enjoying vase-worthy color year-round.

SPRING

MOUNT HOOD DAFFODIL: Durden loves this creamy white variety, softer than the traditional yellow. Plant once and the bulbs will produce flowers year after year. The stems produce a toxin that can be harmful to other cut flowers, though, so soak them overnight before including in mixed arrangements.

SARAH BERNHARDT PEONY: This variety has been around for more than a hundred years and remains a favorite among Southern gardeners. You can cut peonies when they are in bud form and store them in the refrigerator until you need them. Take them out, recut the stems, and they will bloom within a day after being placed in a vase with water—ready to wow dinner guests.

SUMMER

CUT AND COME AGAIN ZINNIA: Durden calls this variety the true cutting flower: The more you cut them, the more they bloom—in all their gorgeous pink, rose, magenta, scarlet, orange, yellow, and cream glory. If you want something more old-fashioned, plant Envy zinnias, which have a chartreuse bloom.

STARGAZER LILY: Unlike other lilies, the ultra-fragrant Stargazer opens up to look at the sky, with big bright pink petals edged with white. *Tip:* Use a damp paper towel to remove the pollen-coated anthers (they spring from the center of the bloom like antennae), which can stain clothing and table linens when they drop.

FALL

LITTLE LIME HYDRANGEA: About a third of the size of a traditional hydrangea, this newer "dwarf" variety is ideal for simple arrangements, and the soft, greenish-white blooms are a nice surprise when the rest of the garden is fading in the fall. As with all woody-stemmed plants, you should pound the base of the stems before placing them in water, which helps them drink more efficiently and last longer.

HONORINE JOBERT ANEMONE: This hardy heirloom has been gracing gardens since the 1800s and remains a Dixie favorite due to its delicate white blooms with golden centers and contrasting dark green leaves. Give anemones room to spread—they are invasive in the best way—so you'll have plenty to cut from without taking away from the beauty of your garden. The stems are very narrow, so you can stuff a big handful into a vase with a slender throat for a bold centerpiece that doesn't take up much table space.

WINTER

LENTEN ROSES: Don't be fooled, these aren't really roses at all. These bright-colored cup-shaped flowers are flanked by evergreen foliage, which makes for a festive arrangement when they bloom from the holidays through early spring. Because colors range from white to deep black-purple—there are literally hundreds of varieties—buy a plant with slightly opened blooms so you know what you're getting. Plant in rich soil with shade, and arrange the flowers in a small bouquet or float several in a shallow dish of water.

VARIEGATED ENGLISH HOLLY: The leaves on this holly plant have white margins, so they really stand out in holiday arrangements. However, they only grow well in the mid and upper South, so ask your local florist which holly variety is best for your area. *Tip*: There are male and female hollies. If you want your plant to produce berries, be sure to plant one of each sex in close proximity.

STOCKING YOUR HOME LIBRARY

"A HOUSE WITHOUT BOOKS is like a room without windows," wrote the great nineteenth-century education reformer Horace Mann. Thankfully, there's no shortage of great books to choose from when it comes to letting a little Southern light into your home.

In literary Oxford, Mississippi, you can't swing a spectacled cat, as they say, without hitting a book nerd. And if you're in the city's legendary Square Books, chances are you're a book nerd, so watch out for those cats. Richard Howorth runs the store—and, as a former mayor, once ran the city at the same time—so who better to recommend some excellent Southern tomes for your shelves? An eminent Oxford bibliophile is going to know a lot about Faulkner, of course, but Howorth's list of five essential Southern books showcases some lesser-known but equally important voices.

Let Us Now Praise Famous Men
BY JAMES AGEE AND WALKER EVANS (1941)

"An American classic, written by Agee with photographs by Evans, that documents the lives of three tenant-farmer families. It was published the same year as William Alexander Percy's *Lanterns on the Levee* and W. J. Cash's *The Mind of the South*, two other giant intellectual histories of the region. No other book captures so vividly the stark realities of the Depression-era rural South."

The Moviegoer

BY WALKER PERCY (1961)

"The great writer's first book and one that I have always called the first Southern postmodern novel. So unlike anything of its time—and winner of the National Book Award for fiction, when two of the other finalists were Joseph Heller's *Catch-22* and Richard Yates's *Revolutionary Road*."

The Complete Stories

BY FLANNERY O'CONNOR (1971)

" 'Whenever I'm asked why Southern writers particularly have a penchant for writing about freaks, I say it is because we are still able to recognize one,' O'Connor famously remarked, and throughout her stories she consistently demonstrates that penchant as well as the sense of humor expressed in the comment. She died at thirty-nine, nearly fifty years ago, her work admired by writers such as Harry Crews and Larry Brown, among others."

All God's Dangers: The Life of Nate Shaw

BY THEODORE ROSENGARTEN (1974)

"Rosengarten was a graduate student doing research in Alabama on Southern sharecroppers' unions of the 1930s when he came across Nate Shaw, an elderly black man who, though illiterate, had committed to memory, and could recount in Homeric style, the stories of his life, encompassing economy, agriculture, labor, race, and every other aspect of Southern society. Winner of the 1975 National Book Award, it's the book I reach for when asked, 'Would you recommend just one book that explains the South?' "

Long, Last, Happy

BY BARRY HANNAH (2010)

"Hannah's innovative style—marked by an outrageous sense of humor and acrobatic, minimalist wordplay—often drew comparisons not to the work of other writers but to that of musicians such as Jimi Hendrix and Miles Davis. Published about a year after his death, this is an excellent selection from his story collections, including many from his classic *Airships*."

ROPE SWING IOI

FEW THINGS BRING OUT your inner kid as easily as the humble rope swing. Passing the lazy days of summer gliding over a cool swimming hole or a shady patch of earth is a memory many Southerners hold dear. But if the rope is not hung right, or the branch supporting it is flimsy, the fun tends to end real quick. To keep things safe, take a few tips from Chris Vaughn, an expert on forestry and land protection with Ducks Unlimited—and, most important, a father who grew up swinging from trees himself.

The first rule of rope-swing hitchin': Choose your tree wisely. Vaughn suggests seeking out oaks: water, cherrybark, willow, the laurels. "All those white and red oaks have the right growth patterns for stout, lower-hanging limbs," he says. "Avoid pines. As we say in forestry, pine is a good 'self-pruning' tree. When lower pine limbs get shaded out, they basically fall off."

Test your branch by thumping it with a thick stick (it should sound "alive" and not hollow), and overengineer everything. "The tree and the rope have to support many times your weight when you're swinging," Vaughn says. Your rope should be at least five-eighths of an inch thick, or, even better, three-fourths. Weatherproof twelve-strand polyolefin wrapped in polyester is both hardier and easier to hang on to than natural twisted-braid rope. And be sure to melt the ends of the cut rope to keep it from unraveling.

To huck the rope over your well-selected branch, tie a double or running bowline knot (a sturdy, broad form of slipknot that won't choke your branch as it grows). "Slip a stick or rock into it, heave it up, and get out of the way," Vaughn says. Then run the knot all the way up and set it by hanging and bouncing from it.

Leave a few extra feet in the rope for tying knots, which will help people of all sizes grip the swing. Finally, if you choose to attach a tire, hitch it on with another bowline knot. "You'll also want to drill holes in the bottom of the tire to drain water," Vaughn says. (Modern radial tires hide sharp steel belting, so use an older bias-style tire or a "tire" from a playground-equipment company.) "And if you plan to swing over water, for God's sake, thoroughly explore the bottom to make sure there are no stumps, cars, or grocery carts. You want your water at least eight feet deep." If water levels are apt to fluctuate, set up a depth gauge on a pole to let kids—or kids at heart—know when it's safe to make a splash.

EAT YOUR KUDZU

SINCE HITTING THE United States in the late nineteenth century, kudzu has been on a rampage. This particularly invasive species was introduced as an ornamental due to its beautiful, sweet-smelling flowers, but kudzu's eventual widespread use for erosion control has had disastrous consequences. In its native southeastern China and southern Japan, insects help keep the broad-leafed vine in check. Not so in the South, where it has no such natural enemies. "The green plague," as it's sometimes called, luxuriates in our sultry climes and propagates like mad, growing up to a foot a day and strangling and smothering other contenders for sun and soil—while providing a great haven for snakes.

There are, however, a few things you can do to tame this wildest of weeds. Many farmers plow the plant and its fat rhizomes under, turning them into nitrogen-rich, manure-replacing fertilizer. Some folks pasture goats on it, eventually eradicating the vine (and getting good milk and wool in the process). But if you can't beat it, eat it. "In Japan, this country creeper is a cure-all, used in medicinal teas and fine cuisine," says Carole Marsh, author of *The Kudzu Cookbook*. Marsh's recipes include frying the leaves like okra, cooking them down like collards, working them into gumbo, and pairing them with Georgia's beloved state vegetable: the sweet Vidalia onion.

Baked Vidalia Onions with Kudzu

6 large **Vidalias,** peeled
1 stick **butter**
Kudzu leaves
Garlic salt
Pepper

SLICE VIDALIAS almost all the way through, in a cross pattern. Insert pats of butter between each section. Roll small, tender kudzu leaves into long, slender pipes and insert in each section. Sprinkle all with garlic salt and pepper. Dot with more butter. Place in a shallow pan filled with water about an inch deep. Cover with foil and bake at 350 degrees for about 30 minutes, or until onions are tender. You can remove the foil and sprinkle with garlic-buttered bread crumbs and continue to bake until set or slightly browned. Serve hot and steaming.

HOW TO MAKE TABBY

UNLESS YOU LIVE NEAR Beaufort, South Carolina, or one of the surrounding Sea Islands off the Georgia and South Carolina coasts, there's a good chance you've never heard of tabby. A slurry of oyster shells, lime, sand, and water, tabby is a rudimentary concrete that was used by the region's early British settlers for home building. Clay was scarce on the islands and bricks too expensive to transport, so colonists looked to their immediate environment for a solution. Oyster shells were procured from Native American kitchen middens or area creeks, and the shells and sand were cleaned to remove any salt, which could weaken the mixture. The shells were then burned to extract the lime, water was added, and the tabby was poured into a wooden frame running the length of the wall or foundation. It was typically cast in two-foot-high increments, and once it dried, the frame was raised and another layer poured on top until the desired wall height was reached. A cheap but labor-intensive process.

Today, tabby is used largely for decorative purposes—low garden walls, patios, and driveways. And you can skip burning the oyster shells. Bagged lime or a portland cement substitute can be found at your local hardware store, making for a manageable do-it-yourself project.

The basic tabby formula is equal parts lime (or portland cement), sand, oyster shells, and water. The amount and the size of the wooden frame will vary depending on the scope and size of your project.

Beaufort architect Colin Brooker, who specializes in preserving and restoring the region's tabby architecture, recommends a lime-based tabby recipe for a more authentic look and a white (not gray) portland cement–based recipe for load-bearing projects such as driveways—it won't yield as rich a patina but is significantly stronger than its lime counterpart. Hit a builders' supply source for sand sold in bulk for children's playgrounds, which is already salt free. Obtaining oyster shells is a bit trickier. Don't go raiding local oyster beds. The Department of Natural Resources tends to frown on such activities. You can try your local seafood purveyor for cast-off shells, but really, why not invite a few dozen of your closest friends over for a good old-fashioned oyster roast. Save the shells, and toast the project with a cold beer.

With your materials assembled, wash the oyster shells thoroughly and then mix the supplies in equal measure. (Note: When using lime, follow any safety precautions printed on the bag.) Brooker recommends crushing a portion of the shells for a better-looking texture. Crush, mix, pour. Repeat.

A SOUTHERN WREATH

COTTON DOESN'T COVER the South as it once did. But if you find yourself on a country road in the old Cotton Belt, there's still a good chance you'll pass at least one cotton field, if not a few miles' worth of fields. It's a striking scene, especially if you happen to be hitting the road in August or September, when the fish are jumpin' and the cotton is high.

Though it's not a good idea to go picking cotton from a stranger's field (it is still a business, after all), there are some online stores where you can source good stems, and local floral shops often stock it. Cotton keeps well and looks beautiful styled in large glass hurricanes, or as a single stem in a small bud vase. But with just a touch of crafting, you can also turn it into a stunning, and very Southern, alternative to the usual wreath. Hang it on your door during the harvest season and leave it up for the holidays.

MATERIALS:

Wreath form (wire or grapevine, depending on preference)

Floral wire

As much **raw cotton** as you can get your hands on

DIRECTIONS:

STEP 1: Wire together 2 to 4 stalks of the raw cotton to create several 10-to-12-inch-long bunches. Be sure to leave enough cotton unbundled to fill out your wreath later.

STEP 2: Gradually working your way around the wreath form, attach a bunch at a time using the floral wire until the surface is more or less covered.

STEP 3: Cut the remaining unbundled stalks and use individual bolls to fill gaps and holes—if you're using a grapevine wreath form, you should be able to tuck these smaller pieces directly into the wreath without securing them with wire.

STEP 4: Embellish with ribbon or foraged flora of your choice.

SILVER WITH A PROPER SHINE

SINCE THE FIRST British settlers brought their silver teapots to the New World, the malleable metal has held a vaunted place on the Southern table. But though it might be called the good silver, these days it's usually punished by being squirreled away to tarnish in obscurity. That is, until a dinner party rolls around and you're faced with a bunch of ugly black place settings the night (or hour) before guests arrive, throwing you into a polishing frenzy.

Charleston, South Carolina–based master silversmith Alfred L. Crabtree, Jr., who has worked with priceless silver everywhere from the High Museum of Art in Atlanta to the Metropolitan Museum of Art in New York, admits that keeping up with your silver in the Southern climate, especially in coastal regions, can be a challenge. Even so, resist the urge to employ shortcuts like harmful chemical dips or even "all-natural" methods like the tin-foil trick—in which silver is bathed in a combination of baking soda, salt, and hot water in a foil-lined sink— which can be particularly damaging to silver-plated pieces. Instead, a little care up front can save you a bigger hassle later.

To state the obvious: Don't wait until your silver turns black. Catch it early. "As soon as it turns a slight golden color, it's time to polish," Crabtree says. "At this stage, you will be able to wipe it off easily." Just run under warm water and dry with a soft cloth. You can use a bit of dish soap, if necessary. But in the event that you do let your silver go black—it happens to the best of us—opt for a good-quality silver polish such as Hagerty. And get ready to put in some elbow grease.

Proper storage will lengthen the time between polishes, so invest in a few felt silversmith bags, which prevent chemicals in the air from reaching the surface of the pieces. You can usually find them at your local jewelry store.

But the surest way to keep your silver shiny is also the easiest: Use it. Silver doesn't promote the growth of bacteria (which is one reason it was valued as tableware in the first place), so it's a simple matter of rinsing with warm water after each meal, Crabtree says. For goodness' sake, just don't put it in the dishwasher.

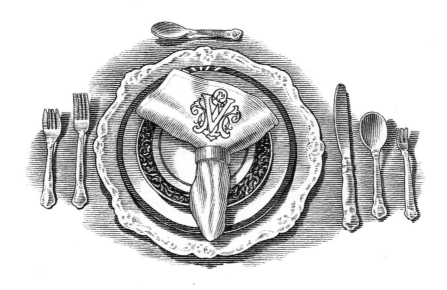

AN HERB GARDEN WITH SOUTHERN ROOTS

AFTER NEARLY FIFTEEN years as head chef at Walland, Tennessee's Blackberry Farm, John Fleer moved across the mountains to Canyon Kitchen, a little restaurant tucked into a North Carolina box canyon, where he has continued to turn out his own brand of upscale rustic fare made with fresh, local ingredients. Canyon Kitchen, like Blackberry Farm, boasts a kitchen garden full of vegetables, yes, but also herbs that Fleer draws on when composing his menus. Stalwarts such as mint and dill are no-brainers, but Fleer also recommends these five favorites for the home cook.

1. ANISE HYSSOP: "Though not the most common herb, this grows right outside the back door of Canyon Kitchen. It adds a wonderful sweet anise flavor to all kinds of desserts. I like to infuse it into hot milk, blend it with buttermilk and simple syrup, and freeze it to make ice milk. A couple of sprigs are amazing in macerated summer berries—blackberries, especially."

2. ITALIAN PARSLEY: "A little bit of Italian parsley is the ultimate way to brighten up a dish. I like to add it in two stages, as I do with most soft herbs. First at the beginning of cooking, for maximum flavor, and then at the end, to achieve that unmistakable freshness. My favorite use for Italian parsley is as a whole leaf in salad, especially paired

with lemon zest, olive oil, and sea salt and served on seared rainbow trout."

3. LEMON VERBENA: "Some people say that lemon verbena smells like furniture polish, but I think that its seductive aroma works wonders muddled or infused into cocktails, summer sodas, or punches. It can transport a refreshing gin and tonic to another realm."

4. TARRAGON: "For those of us living in the mid-South, the return of this herb is a sign that spring is upon us. Tarragon is outstanding with new creamer potatoes, lightly roasted or used to make a creamy spring potato soup."

5. THYME: "Thyme adds the base note to much of my cooking. Essential in cold-weather braises, it also adds depth to brighter preparations like summer succotash. A touch of thyme in a vegetable side dish complements rich, meaty main courses like ribs or roasted pork shoulder."

MAN VS. WEED

BY ROY BLOUNT, JR.

WHEN A PERSON IS—and by that I mean thank heaven she is—allowing a fellow to share his life, I mean her life, I mean their life, with her, she may sometimes ask the fellow in question, out of the blue, "Would you like a little project?"

In such an instance, I believe I speak for most fellows when I say that the fellow's manly and straightforward answer is "No."

Manly, straightforward, but not audible. If there is one thing that a person who is allowing a fellow to share his life with her holds to be self-evident, it is this: that he is *not* sharing if he is relaxing.

I mean, a fellow knows that in her graciousness she will not necessarily throw scalding grits all over him or run off with the mailman, but a fellow also knows that if he were to give in automatically to his own frame of reference (which may be bounded at the moment by a sporting event thousands of miles away), he would risk doing something inexplicable in her eyes. Can he ever reject a little project, from the heart, without declaring in effect that he is veering dangerously close to perceivably courting estrangement?

No. That is far from the kind of peril that quickens a fellow's blood. But what if the light of his life were to come running in yelling something along the lines of "Lordy Lordy, we are about to be swallowed up by the phragmites!"? Then a fellow would be inclined to leap into action, at least at the conclusion of this series of downs. A fellow needs a heroic mission, an epic mission. And if there is any area of domestic life where this principle applies, it is gardening.

Don't get me wrong, I enjoy poking around in our garden and yard quite undramatically. Random weeding, inspection of compost, woodpile micromanagement: These pursuits do support, at least arguably, the domestic enterprise. So they free a fellow up to think about something else. Surely the expression "woolgathering" derives from the serious, if, okay, piddling, pursuit of gathering, here and there, odd tufts of wool. To . . . do something with.

But piddling does not fully satisfy a fellow. He needs a cause, a grievance, a battle to the wire.

And so I treasure my fight against the invasive weed phragmites. The very name, *phragmites,* combines *frag, rag,* and *mighty.* The plant is a colonizer. It crowds out native species. Granted, you could call that a great American story, but not these days. After Hurricane Irene burst the dam upriver from our house, phragmites began to show up along the bank that borders our yard. Phragmites is perhaps less galloping than kudzu, but it can grow much taller: up to sixteen feet

high, without attaching itself to anything. The *phrag* part comes from the Greek for *fence* or *hedge.* Phragmites wants to block our view of the river, so that we can't watch ducks and the occasional great blue heron from our kitchen window. We *like* watching ducks and the occasional great blue heron. And think about this: What is phragmites concealing behind that hedge? Maybe something *worse,* for which phragmites is a stalking horse. At any rate, phragmites grounds itself terrorist-like in ugly aggressive rhizome systems. Oh, to a phragmites these bulbous tentacle-looking clumps may seem cute and deservedly self-assured. To me they are right down a fellow's alley: something to be killed without compunction.

So seizing my stouthearted spade, Hrothgar the Not Very Rusty, I hew phragmites stalk and branch; I smite phragmites at its very rhizomatous shoot-and-root fundament; I heave phragmites by main force from the ground; and . . . that, to me, is gardening. Nor is my wrath unrighteous, for not only can phragmites block views of likable nature, and eat up riparian real estate, and maybe abduct slow-moving pets, it also flaunts itself rather shamelessly. I quote Wikipedia: "inflorescence conspicuous, large, . . . plume-like, . . . silky, . . . often draping to one side, many ascending branches, ring of hairs at base; . . . stalks hairy."

Indeed, there are documented accounts of phragmites audibly *snickering* at valiant gardeners who . . . maybe not *documented* documented, and maybe *audibly* is too strong a word, but then see paragraph three. Ask any fellow who has pitted himself against this silky, sneering menace: Phragmites is out to destroy our way of life. Inside heavy black trash bags is where it belongs.

Part Six

ARTS & CULTURE

THE ART OF PLACE

BY ALLISON GLOCK

*I*N MY OFFICE I KEEP A CERAMIC SILVER SWAN. IT IS ABOUT THE SIZE OF A BASEBALL, HOLLOWED OUT BETWEEN THE WINGS, WHERE I'VE INSERTED A CANDLE I HAVE YET TO LIGHT. ON THE UNDERSIDE OF THE BIRD, SWIMMING IN THE CENTER OF PLAIN WHITE GLAZING, IS MY GREAT-GRANDFATHER'S STAMP. "DECORATED BY A. C. BLAIR, CHESTER, W. VA." LIKE THE BEAK, THE STAMP IS PAINTED IN LIQUID GOLD.

Of all my many relatives who worked in the pottery factories of West Virginia, Andrew Blair was the most artistic. Over the years, he toiled his way up from repetitive line labor to a slightly less repetitive decorator's position—lining mug rims with the popular colors of the day, detailing vases with flowers and kittens.

When he came home from his shift, he'd head to the garden shed, where he'd set up his own hand-cranked potter's wheel, a circle of marble that sat on top of a cast-iron stand. There, Andrew would spin plates and hand-paint them with ballerinas, or gurgling infants, or customized logos for local businesses like the VFW. He labeled each piece with his gold signature, or sometimes just "Blairware." But he never considered himself an artist. He was a poor father of five children who needed to earn every way he could. His gift was irrelevant.

So it has been for much of the South's creative history. Southern art, like all great things Southern, sprang from necessity. Utilitarian craftsmanship honed to exquisite singularity out of need, not ego. Hobbies that filled the hours. Or that particular heat-induced madness that leads one to paint polka dots on every surface of one's house, or compulsively carve angels and scrawl Scripture across their faces. Southerners are loath, even now, to claim the title of artiste outright. It feels uppity. Disconnected. Not of the land. Not part of history.

I know dozens of Southern writers who blanch when asked what they do for a living. Most refuse to answer, "I'm a writer," for fear of sounding ridiculous. Writing is a verb, after all. Not a profession.

Legendary Appalachian craftsman Alex Stewart didn't whittle extraordinary wildlife dioramas to make "sculpture." It was something he used to kill time when he found himself too old to do what he labeled "worthwhile things."

Louis Armstrong declared, "All music is folk music." Ragtime, bluegrass, gospel, blues, country, soul—genres born in the South to the same invisible, underclass mother. "What we play is life," he explained. The roots of our music, like all our art, share a melancholy yearning, an ache to be heard and *felt*, never to dazzle or impress. (Perhaps that's why so many Southern painters claim to be compelled by the Holy Spirit to create. No one can argue with God's work.)

Thing is, when you come from the bayou or the holler or the fields, folks don't expect much. They sure as hell don't expect *culture*. And so began a long tradition of regional dismissal by outsiders. And a habit of diminishing ourselves. Of course, being Southerners, we figured out a way to be heard anyway. We told stories.

We told our stories with humor and vicious heart and volume. We sang about sex and called it rock and roll. We painted devils you could fall in love with. We wrote (and wrote and wrote) in feral tongues with unprecedented vulnerability and transparency, and in doing all this, we wriggled in and rearranged your insides and made you see us, the real us, because, above all, Southern art is not something you can hide from. It will make you look. And you will be forever changed as a result.

Which is what the truth does. And what real art does.

Even if we never call it that.

SOUTHERNISMS

BY DANIEL WALLACE

SOUTHERN COLLOQUIAL expressions (as my pappy used to say in his down-home way) are multifarious and, in fact, possibly infinite. Most of them mention animals, often dogs. For example:

"That dog won't hunt."

"That's a hard dog to keep on the porch."

"You ain't nothin' but a hound dog."

"Run with the big dogs or stay on the porch."

"Happy as a tick on a fat dog."

Et cetera. Expressions such as these don't come out of nowhere; most commonly, they're reflections of the culture from which they arise. In this case, it's clear that dogs are integral to the South and the character of its people. Is it even possible to be Southern and *not* have a dog—probably many dogs? No. If you don't have dogs, if you don't *love* dogs, you have come from somewhere else and are just pretending to be Southern, probably to meet women who are really into bad grammar and droppin' *g*'s.

There are other animals commonly referred to in Southernisms as well, including but not limited to cats, turtles, gators, birds, possums, and skunks. Nature—trees, for instance—is important and makes a number of appearances, as in "lit up like a Christmas tree." And then there are some with both dogs *and* trees. "It's so hot I saw two trees fighting over a dog," for instance.

Within these general guidelines, it's

possible to create your own Southernisms, expressions that one day might find their way into the common parlance. Here are a few I've made up myself:

"Lonely as a pine tree in a parking lot."

"Funny as a three-legged dog in a horse race."

"Give him two nickels for a dime and he'll think he's rich."

And here's one that seems likely to enter the lexicon any minute now: "That cat won't hunt."

TEN LIVELY EXPRESSIONS

"ALL HAT, NO CATTLE"

Imagine the would-be ranching magnate, flush with cash earned elsewhere, who blows into town with a ten-gallon lid, a fresh pair of boots—and a much too loud mouth.

"DRUNKER THAN COOTER BROWN"

As legend has it, Cooter Brown was a man who did not see fit to take up with either side during the Civil War, and so remained so staggeringly drunk throughout the entire conflict that he avoided conscription.

"FINE AS FROG'S HAIR SPLIT FOUR WAYS"

What's that? You've never seen hair on a frog? Exactly. Split it four ways and it becomes awfully fine indeed.

"GRINNING LIKE A POSSUM EATING A SWEET POTATO"

For a scavenger accustomed to a diet of bugs, slugs, and roadkill, having a fat, juicy sweet potato to gorge on is like winning the lottery.

"HAPPY AS A DEAD PIG IN THE SUNSHINE"

Deceptively complex, this one contains a built-in lesson in postmortem porcine physiology. As a dead pig's body lies out in the sunshine, see, its lips begin to pull back from its teeth, creating the illusion of a wide grin. The expression describes a similarly oblivious (though quite alive) person who smiles away when in reality things aren't going so hot.

"KNEE-HIGH TO A GRASSHOPPER"

Most often used to denote growth, as in: "I haven't seen you since you were knee-high to a grasshopper!"

"SLOWER THAN MOLASSES RUNNING UPHILL IN THE WINTER"

Things don't get much slower than molasses. Uphill in winter? You get the picture.

"RAN LIKE A SCALDED HAINT"

The opposite meaning of the previous phrase. A haint, in old Southern terminology, is a ghost, and according to tradition, scalding one will send it running right quick.

"LIKE A CAT ON A HOT TIN ROOF"

Cats are jumpy enough in a comfortable living room. The expression describes someone in an extreme state of upset and anxiety, and, of course, it was used by Tennessee Williams as the title of his Pulitzer-winning 1955 play.

"ENOUGH MONEY TO BURN A WET MULE"

Why a person might choose to burn a soaking wet thousand-pound mule is anybody's guess, but the expression was made famous (in some circles) when legendary Louisiana governor Huey Long used it in reference to deep-pocketed nemesis Standard Oil.

SONGS OF THE SOUTH

BY DONOVAN WEBSTER

WHY HERE? How do you explain all the great music that's come out of the American South and—in not much more than a century—shocked, inspired, and changed the sound of pretty much every other culture on earth? Name another region anywhere, ever, that's brought forth so much great music in so many styles. Music that continues to multiply and evolve and open our ears to new forms.

You can't.

Jazz? It's from New Orleans. Gospel? The South alone. The blues? The Mississippi Delta. Bluegrass and country? Appalachia. Rock and roll? Memphis and environs. No Chess or King R&B without blues and jazz. No Stax or Motown soul without gospel and R&B. No funk without soul and R&B and the influence of New Orleans.

Not to mention the ancestors that never died. Old-time music. Cajun chanky-chank. And the Lowcountry's Gullah tunes, which work like semaphore among those who understand their often subversive meanings.

So much of it goes back to the slave songs, spirituals sung in fields and around hearths. At night, in the rarefied world of the big house, you might have heard a classical quartet playing Haydn, but a life of hardship is what brought soul to church music and midwifed jazz and the blues, which was just more rhythm and perhaps a secondary melody.

Muddy Waters was born in Jug's Corner, Mississippi, and his heroes were the Delta bluesmen Son House and Robert Johnson. I once had the honor of sitting down to a meal with the man, and though

I've misplaced or lost the notes I made at the time, I'll never forget what he told me. He asked if I knew what a gospel or blues song was. He explained that it was good rhythm, a working person's rhythm—and if it's the blues, a good guitar line. Then, he said, all you need are words and a story. At that he looked down, pointed to the knife on the table, and talked about how you could cook with it, cut rope with it, or kill a man with it. Right there, he said, you're mostly done writing a blues song.

Of course, not *all* American music is from the South. New York City invented big-band jazz and punk—and the Harlem Renaissance took New Orleans jazz and ran with it. Chicago did its thing with the blues, mostly by offering social change and electricity to men from Mississippi. Detroit embraced R&B and soul. The Caribbean and West Africa have played their parts. The British Isles have given, received, and given back to us several times, contributing mightily in waves; our musical cultures have cross-pollinated for centuries.

But the South can claim the new forms born here. I don't think it could've happened anywhere else. It has to do with the rich mix of cultures, from African to Scotch-Irish to, yes, Native American—tribes all. It has to do with a slower pace of life. The music is in the earth, the air, and the water, uniquely of this place.

The arrival of the Scotch-Irish in southern Appalachia in the early 1800s brought with it musical instruments beyond the voice: the violin, mandolin, banjo, tambour, and all-important guitar. The music that came with these folks—ballads, jigs, and reels, their folk music—began to morph as it traveled through the Cumberland Gap. Before too long, there was bluegrass, which has left us with so many great artists: Bill Monroe, the Stanley Brothers, Doc Watson, Flatt & Scruggs.

Then came country music, a new form that slowed down the Celtic-derived stuff, put it in a blues mode, and then went on to pretty much build the city of Nashville with songs about "mama and freight trains and three-legged dogs and broken hearts and prison," in the words of one friend with years in the industry there.

One of my favorite musicians is Hiram King Williams; you probably know him as "Hank," the epitome of country's twang and sorrow. A son of Mount Olive, Alabama, he basically wrote a song a day across his adult life, which unfortunately ended in 1953—when he was just twenty-nine—in the back of a Cadillac somewhere between Bristol, Virginia, and Oak Hill, West Virginia. Hank is said to have remarked that most of his songs were set to the tempo of a beating heart. Music was simply waiting inside him. It often took whiskey to get it out, but it was always there.

After Hank & Co. came the ruffians, the rock and rollers and the soul and R&B singers. Once again, new sounds seemed to just appear fully formed: up-tempo mixes of blues and country and gospel and jazz in different flavors. Out of Louisiana came Jerry Lee Lewis and the Neville Brothers. Little Richard and Otis Redding hailed from Georgia. Elvis Presley from Mississippi, along with Bo Diddley. From Arkansas, Al Green and Johnny Cash. From Tennessee, Carl Perkins and, long before him, the influential Carter Family. James Brown came out of South Carolina. Roy Orbison from Texas. Ike from Mississippi, Tina from Tennessee.

From here on out, Southern music just kept bubbling up and spilling all over the place, mixing old and new cultures and influences and throwing it all into a big stew pot, cooking it down in kitchens and on front porches across the South to later be refined inside now-legendary recording studios like Sun and Stax in Memphis, Cosimo in New Orleans, Chess in Chicago, Motown in Detroit, Muscle Shoals in Alabama.

The music has never stopped, and it

has never stopped evolving. Think of the Southern rock of the Allman Brothers, Lynyrd Skynyrd, Marshall Tucker, Charlie Daniels, Tom Petty, ZZ Top, and Alabama. Just try to definitively categorize Jimmy Buffett (who, as a young songwriter in Nashville, had the dubious honor of being thrashed by famed Tennessee sheriff Buford "Walking Tall" Pusser). And don't you dare forget ladies like June Carter Cash, Loretta Lynn, and Lucinda Williams, who've reshaped Southern music each according to her own beautiful will.

A great example of a younger band finding success—and its way—by staying true to the roots found in this rich earth is North Carolina's Avett Brothers. On a visit to my hometown—Charlottesville, Virginia—in late 2012, the brothers began speaking lovingly of life in the rural South. We were just sitting around, and I had a question. Referencing one of their biggest hits, "I and Love and You," a song that includes the line "Ah Brooklyn, Brooklyn, take me in," I felt compelled to ask, "So Brooklyn didn't take you in?"

The Avetts both chuckled. "It does from time to time," Scott said, "but then it always spits us back out. You know, back down to North Carolina. It's all cool."

That sense of fun and good nature and community is another big part of what makes our music culture so great. It's like our musicians are brothers and sisters, the kind you find in a church. One of my favorite stories comes out of a night in the early 1980s I spent hanging out with the king of rockabilly, Carl Perkins, who grew up hardscrabble near Jackson, Tennessee. On this evening, we were in New York City outside the Mudd Club. He'd just done a show with his sons, on drums and stand-up bass, and they were headed back home on the tour bus. We were talking, and he said he first wrote "Blue Suede Shoes" on the back of a grocery sack. "I was in the kitchen, at the table, with my guitar, and that bag was all I had to write on," he said. "I had one pencil." He then began telling me about Elvis and what a nice guy he was.

"Were you angry he took a song you wrote and recorded, then recorded it himself and made it a big hit?" I asked.

"Son," Carl said, "he became a friend.

And when he did that song—boy, oh, boy—the music totally took him over. That was something I was happy to be a part in." Isn't that what it's really all about—being a part of something that came before you and grows beyond you, something that fills you up and surrounds you?

A few years ago, my son was invited by some friends to an African Baptist Church while he was visiting Charleston, South Carolina. When he got back home, he told me, "The church service lasted all day Sunday, but I didn't mind. The music was always going, and everyone would stop church for a while and eat together, and then they would start church again. And it was . . . *amazing.*"

Exactly.

FIVE ESSENTIAL VENUES

ALTHOUGH SOUTHERN MUSIC was born and raised far from the glare of stage lights, today, much like favorite songs, certain Southern venues have reached iconic status. There are no better places to catch a show than these five stalwarts—except maybe someone's moonlit porch.

little venue has launched the careers of homegrown bands including R.E.M., the B-52s, and the Indigo Girls, and remains a favorite stopover for a slew of national acts. Come to soak up the rock-and-roll history and leave with your ears ringing.

THE 40 WATT CLUB

ATHENS, GEORGIA

The 40 Watt Club has been ground zero for sweaty, beer-soaked Southern rock since it opened more than three decades ago. Named for the flickering 40-watt bulb that lit its earliest iteration, the

THE STATION INN

NASHVILLE, TENNESSEE

When the Station Inn opened in 1974, the surrounding neighborhood—known as the Gulch—was a past-its-prime industrial zone giving in to rust and decay. Today, the neighborhood is better known for luxury condos and trendy restaurants.

But the Station Inn, a squat stone building with boarded-up windows, holds tight to the old days. Dark, crowded, lit by neon signs and papered with old concert posters, it is the no-nonsense home of bluegrass music in Nashville.

RED'S LOUNGE

CLARKSDALE, MISSISSIPPI

Clarksdale has Delta-blues history thick and deep. It was the hometown of legendary preacher turned bluesman Son House. It's where Robert Johnson—according to legend, anyway—sank down at the crossroads and where W. C. Handy, often called the father of the blues, learned his craft. And though the juke joint may be a dying breed these days, the windowless barbecue and juke that is Red's Lounge remains an authentic piece of the town's rich legacy. Just remember the rules hand-painted on the building: no standing outside and no drugs.

THE RYMAN AUDITORIUM

NASHVILLE, TENNESSEE

The onetime Union Gospel Tabernacle attracted faithful hordes of a different sort as the home of the Grand Ole Opry from 1943 to 1974. Rechristened the Ryman Auditorium, it has played host to some of the most important events in country music. Bill Monroe and Earl Scruggs established bluegrass there in the 1940s. Johnny Cash first met—and pledged his love to—June Carter backstage. A young Elvis Presley vowed never to return, according to legend, after a straitlaced Opry official advised him to go back to driving a truck. Although the Grand Ole Opry has moved to a larger facility, the stained-glass windows and Sunday-morning acoustics at the so-called mother church of country music still draw reverent legions of musicians and country-music aficionados.

FRITZEL'S EUROPEAN JAZZ PUB

NEW ORLEANS, LOUISIANA

While it is by no means the most famous jazz venue in New Orleans—that title might go to a more-trafficked spot like Preservation Hall or Tipitina's—you simply must catch a show at this venue, one of the oldest jazz halls in the oldest jazz city in the United States. Tucked away near the residential part of Bourbon Street, Fritzel's is small and intimate, a grown-up bar that caters to artists who still specialize in true Dixieland jazz, with a clientele that does not need to be told to chant the chorus to Cab Calloway's "Minnie the Moocher."

DANCE LIKE A COWBOY

IN PARTS OF TEXAS, a boy or a girl cannot come of age without learning to two-step. And while you may not be from Texas, if you find yourself in a boots-and-beer joint and the floor fills up with dancing cowboys and cowgirls, you do not want to be the solitary wallflower. Keep the two-step—a dance so easy that even a cowboy can do it, as the saying goes—on hand for just such an occasion.

THE POSITION: If you are a man, place your right hand on the woman's left shoulder and hold your left hand out, elbow bent. If you are a woman, take that left hand in your right hand and place your left hand on the man's right biceps.

THE RHYTHM: Rhythm is the key to the two-step. 1, 2, 3-4, 5-6. 1, 2, 3-4, 5-6. Count it off in your head. Or out loud, if you're dancing with an understanding partner.

THE STEPS: The steps go quick-quick, slow-slow—that's a pair of one-beat steps and a pair of two-beat steps. If you're a man, step forward with your left foot first. Women, step back with your right. Then men, forward with the right foot, and women, back with the left. Repeat, pausing on the fourth and sixth beats.

Then do it all again. Work your way counterclockwise around the dance floor, sticking close to the center if you are still a slow-moving beginner. When you get the hang of it, throw a spin or two into your routine. Move with confidence, remaining aware of the dancers around you and, of course, the location of your partner's feet.

THE CHURCH OF SOUTHERN FOOTBALL

AT THE END OF 1925, the little-known University of Alabama football team boarded a train to California to take on the undefeated Washington Huskies in the twelfth Rose Bowl. "Southern football is not recognized or respected," Alabama coach Wallace Wade told his team. "Boys, here's your chance to change that forever."

Defying all expectations, Alabama's football team won the game and established Southern football as a thing to be reckoned with. Today, the teams of the SEC (Southeastern Conference) are both recognized and respected above the Mason-Dixon Line—and worshipped below it. SEC football is its own religion down south, and with passionate football fans, of course, come passionate rivalries. None more heated than these three.

UNIVERSITY OF ALABAMA VS. AUBURN

Though Auburn and Alabama meet only once a year, at the Iron Bowl, the tension between the two schools has run high year-round for more than a century. Their very first game, which Auburn won, was marred by a dispute over whether it should be counted as part of the 1892 or 1893 season. After a tied game in 1907, the heads of both institutions decided that their football teams should stop playing each other. And so they did, until the state house stepped in—yes, the state house—and issued a 1947 resolution that pushed them back into the fray. The game is now a Thanksgiving weekend tradition.

UNIVERSITY OF FLORIDA VS. UNIVERSITY OF GEORGIA

Though the rivalry itself is fierce, the tailgating might be even fiercer. The annual game between the Florida Gators and the Georgia Bulldogs is known as the "World's Largest Outdoor Cocktail Party," and it draws hordes of rowdy spectators to Jacksonville, Florida. Why Jacksonville? It was chosen as a "neutral" location back in 1915, and with rare exception, the game has been played there every year since 1933. Apart from a whole lot of hangovers, generations of football have produced plenty of memorable moments on the field, including what some call the greatest in Georgia football history: Georgia radio announcer Larry Munson's cry of "Run, Lindsay!" as wide receiver Lindsay Scott hustled to the end zone for an unprecedented—and game-winning—92-yard touchdown in 1980.

MISSISSIPPI STATE VS. UNIVERSITY OF MISSISSIPPI

Neither Mississippi State nor Ole Miss competes at the level of some of the other SEC schools, but that doesn't mean their rivalry is any less intense. Back in 1926, after losing thirteen straight against Mississippi A&M (now Mississippi State), Ole Miss squeaked out a one-point victory in the two teams' annual matchup. Ole Miss fans went wild, rushing the field and trying to tear down A&M's goalposts, and the scene soon devolved into chaos. As the A&M yearbook put it, "A few chairs had to be sacrificed over the heads of these to persuade them that was entirely the wrong attitude." Looking to bring some dignity back to the game, the schools introduced the Golden Egg, a spheroid trophy modeled after what was then a regulation football. And ever since, the Battle for the Golden Egg, usually just called the Egg Bowl, has determined football dominance in Mississippi—no chair sacrificing required.

THE CROWDED CANON OF THE SOUTH

BY HAL ESPEN

THE MOST TALISMANIC literary object I own is a fine first edition of William Faulkner's 1936 novel *Absalom, Absalom!*, a shockingly expensive thing when I bought it as a dirt-poor college student several decades back. It's routinely esteemed as the greatest Southern novel ever written, and sometimes called the only rival to Melville's *Moby-Dick* as that rough beast, the Great American You-Know-What. *Absalom* radiates the kind of preemptive, Book of Genesis force that the Milledgeville, Georgia, peacock fancier Flannery O'Connor was talking about when she famously described the challenge of writing in Yoknapatawpha's wake: "Nobody wants his mule and wagon stalled on the same track the Dixie Limited is roaring down."

Genius intimidates, it's true. But it also enlarges. The Southern genius of Faulkner, Eudora Welty, Zora Neale Hurston, Richard Wright, Tennessee Williams, and O'Connor herself—not to mention Louis Armstrong, Robert Johnson, Elvis, and Ray Charles—stomped giant footprints across a mythic territory that hadn't quite existed, but it subsequently gave us a matchless American inheritance. The critic Northrop Frye argued that the region—rather than one's nation or any mere political geography—is the imagination's true home, and our supreme metaregionalism has been (and I'd argue still is) the Southern lit'ry tradition.

Taking as our nominal epoch the years since Faulkner died, in 1962, let's shine a light on the best of what Southern writers—particularly novelists—have done to explore this territory and enrich its bequest in the wake of the Dixie Limited.

During the sixties, a decade whose apocalyptic unruliness transformed the South, Southern writers showed up with their own brace of bombshells: Truman Capote's 1966 "nonfiction novel" *In Cold Blood* and William Styron's blackface-revolutionary *The Confessions of Nat Turner* (1967). The era's less explosive masterworks include *The Moviegoer*, Walker Percy's New Orleans–based 1961 gem; *A Long and Happy Life* (1962), which launched Reynolds Price's distinguished career; and 1966's *Norwood* and '68's *True Grit*, the first two novels by the sublime Arkansas craftsman Charles Portis. In 1969, John Kennedy Toole, the patron saint of rejected writers, took his own life, but posthumous vindication came when his own picaresque and dangerously funny New Orleans novel, *A Confederacy of Dunces*, was published in 1980 and won the Pulitzer Prize.

The sixties and seventies saw the emergence of Wendell Berry, the South's foremost voice of dissent and moral philosophy since Martin Luther King, Jr. His extraordinary output of essays, poetry, and fiction includes many vibrant works based in the imagined town of Port William, Kentucky. *The Memory of Old Jack* (1999), perhaps Berry's finest novel, is a beautiful way to discover this agrarian prophet. Berry's opposite in almost every way but residence in Kentucky and literary stature was the spiky, classics-besotted modernist Guy Davenport. He came of age valuing Samuel Beckett and Eudora Welty as the greatest living writers, and he produced dazzlingly Joycean stories and essays with barely a Southern accent, often featuring a time-travel mash-up of antiquity and the contemporary. *Twelve Stories* (1997) is a superb point of entry.

The seventies rumbled in with James Dickey's ultraviolent *Deliverance* (1970), and the lunatic splendor and slashing edges of Georgian-Floridian Harry Crews's *A Feast of Snakes* (1976) heralded the Dirty South lit to come. Three years later came *Suttree*, the last purely Southern (and first purely great) novel by Cormac McCarthy before he decamped to southwestern settings. This was also the heyday of Barry Hannah, a tragicomic jester who could do with sentences what Duane Allman did with electric slide-guitar licks; the Mississippi madness of *Ray*, his 1980 novel, is nonpareil.

The similarly wondrous humor of Padgett Powell's debut novel, *Edisto* (1984), kept Southern precocity spinning apace. The eighties also witnessed a near-miraculous breakout of brilliant Southern women writers. *The Color Purple*, Alice Walker's 1982 novel, stands alongside semi-Southerner Toni Morrison's *Beloved* (1987) at the pinnacle of fiction about the African American experience. Other signature distaff-side achievements of the day: *Oral History*, by the great Appalachian storyteller Lee Smith (1983); *In Country*, by Bobbie Ann Mason (1985); *Ellen Foster*, by Kaye Gibbons (1987); and *Rich in Love*, by Josephine Humphreys (1988). And with *Trash*, her 1988 collection of stories, and *Bastard Out of Carolina*, her 1992 novel, Dorothy Allison distilled a lacerating and low-down Southern fearlessness.

Landmarks of the twentieth century's ultimate decade include *A Lesson Before Dying*, Ernest J. Gaines's widely adored 1993 novel, set in a 1940s Cajun community; Pinckney Benedict's noirish *Dogs of God* (1993); Larry Brown's gorgeously uglified *Father and Son* (1996); and Sharyn McCrumb's *The Ballad of Frankie Silver* (1999), one of her best literary mysteries. Among the new millennium's arrivals in the pantheon is *The Known World*, Edward P. Jones's 2004 Pulitzer winner, set in antebellum Virginia.

A shout-out to the South's crime thrillers—especially those set in sin-soaked Florida—is mandatory: John D. MacDonald's state-of-the-art Travis McGee series (1964 to 1984); stunners by Charles Willeford (*Miami Blues*) and honorary Southerner Elmore Leonard (*LaBrava* and *Maximum Bob*, for example); the deranged entertainments of Carl Hiaasen (*Lucky You*, *Skinny Dip*, etc.). These tales of extremely bad behavior in the Sunshine State are national treasures.

A list two, three times longer than this should still go straight to hell for mortal sins of omission. Southern loquacity cries out for justice! Where are Clyde Edgerton, T. R. Pearson, Larry McMurtry, Ann Patchett? For God's sake, what about the poets: Dave Smith, Al Young, Rita Dove? The humorists, like that deadly wit Roy

Blount, Jr.? Or essayists like the great Annie Dillard, who go-go danced with Lee Smith back at Hollins College (now Hollins University) in a sixties rock band called the Virginia Woolfs? All those Southern-fried plays and screenplays? And let's don't even get started on the historical and nonfiction works, from Shelby Foote's Gibbonesque multivolume *The Civil War: A Narrative* to *Midnight in the Garden of Good and Evil,* by John Berendt (1994)—sadly, a New York Yankee. This tradition continues with *The Warmth of Other Suns* (2010), in which Isabel Wilkerson, a daughter of D.C. with Georgia and Virginia roots, tells the epic story of the twentieth century's great African American migration to northern and western metropolises, which swept Southern-born John Coltrane and Ralph Ellison and Muddy Waters and so many others toward their American apotheoses.

Amid this too-muchness of a past that's not even past, we keep a sharp lookout for whatever's coming next from the South's twanging pens. Come it will. "It's a good bloodline, and one must be from a bloodline," Padgett Powell once averred of his literary pedigree. "To paraphrase a dogfighter I know, them Southern dogs is hell, ain't they?"

THE TRUTH ABOUT
ROBERT JOHNSON AND THE DEVIL
BY ACE ATKINS

IN THE CLASSIC WESTERN *The Man Who Shot Liberty Valance*, Jimmy Stewart confesses to a newspaperman that he did not, in fact, shoot the title's infamous outlaw, as most believe. The effort to set the record straight and give proper credit backfires, and the newspaperman refuses to retell the story, uttering the famous lines "This is the West, sir. When the legend becomes fact, print the legend."

The same can be said of the South and the sometimes tall tales obscuring its greatest heroes—none more famous than the story of Robert Johnson. But this time, let's not give in to the legend.

Robert Johnson is the revolutionary bluesman who, we've been told, went to Clarksdale, Mississippi, and sold his soul to the devil at the crossroads of Highways 61 and 49, in exchange for superhuman guitar skills. (No mention is made of his incredible singing voice.) We've also been told that this deal sealed Johnson's fate and led to his death by poisoning at a juke joint near Greenwood, Mississippi, in 1938, when he was only twenty-seven.

In his short life, he recorded twenty-nine songs, brilliant poetry and musicianship that ignited such British invaders as the Rolling Stones, Eric Clapton, and Led Zeppelin. Johnson's voice is powerful, resonant, and eerie, with pitch control that does feel almost supernatural—a cold wind across the Delta's cotton fields. But that irresistible Faustian tale of Johnson's deal with the devil has rotten roots. It actually has its origins in a 1971 biography of the influential early bluesman *Tommy* Johnson (unrelated), whose brother told author David Evans the tale of a bargain with the devil. That story was transformed via a later *Rolling Stone* piece by Greil Marcus, who stated that perhaps ol' Bob had sold his soul, too. In the years following, the "perhaps" got knocked off and the legend went viral. (Johnson's seminal "Me and the Devil Blues" didn't help matters.)

Robert Johnson had a good pal and playing partner named Johnny Shines, who laughed off the story in the documentary *The Search for Robert Johnson*, saying, "How does a man sell his soul? Let me see your soul. Hand it over to me." But Johnson's shadowy death seems to be the clincher for most. As the legend has it, Johnson rambles into the cotton town of Greenwood, Mississippi, and ends up playing at a juke called the 3 Forks Store, where the devilishly talented lothario shows some attention to the wife of the owner. The jealous husband laces the young master's whiskey with strychnine.

Johnson takes ill, dying some days later, on August 16, howling like a dog and crying for mercy.

The devil's called in his marker.

But the truth? The strychnine story just doesn't jibe; one would have to consume a fatal dose, and death would be swift. No, Johnson was most likely taken by a disease that was sweeping Mississippi during the Great Depression: syphilis. How do we know? It's written right there, in black and white, on the back of the man's death certificate, which was unearthed by famed blues researcher Gayle Dean Wardlow decades ago. Wardlow and I met up in Greenwood in 2001 after rumors surfaced that a woman still living in the area had witnessed Johnson's burial.

Rosie Eskridge, then in her eighties, was a wizened old woman, sharp as they get, and had spent most of her life living on the Star of the West plantation, north of Greenwood along Money Road. She was a new discovery—a fortunate find during a lawsuit between Robert Johnson's son and the Johnson estate—and she pointed out where a small house once stood next door. It had been inhabited by a man she called "Tush Hog" and several of his daughters. One of the daughters, Eskridge said, took up with a traveling musician who got sick, was laid up in the house for a while, and died.

How'd you know it was Robert Johnson?

"I never said his name," she said. "I only know it was August of '38 and the man who died played guitar."

How can you be sure of the date?

"I know it was August. It was hot. I know it was '38, getting out of the Depression and a few years before the war."

Eskridge recounted how, during those hot August days leading up to the sixteenth, everyone knew about the guitar man who'd taken ill. When he died, the foreman of the plantation called up several men to dig a grave. One of the men was Eskridge's husband.

Who was the foreman?

"Jim Moore"—the name of the "informant" recorded on Robert Johnson's death certificate. Eskridge said there was a juke joint within walking distance of the plantation. She told us her husband dug Johnson's grave by a small church, also within walking distance. "Zion Church" is also on the death certificate.

We rode with Eskridge to the old cemetery at Little Zion and wandered with her through the crooked headstones to the large oak tree where she said the hole was dug. She pointed with her cane at the exact spot, not the place where a headstone was placed years later, and said Johnson had been laid in a cheap pine box provided by the county. No kind words were said, no Bible verses recited. The men just put Johnson in the hole and filled it up.

Eskridge never heard a whisper about foul play.

Some blues fanatics cast doubt on the death certificate's B-side, wondering how many black men were murdered back then with a false cause of death listed on the certificate. But to understand the South is to understand the naked racism of the time. The fact of a murdered black man was reported, not hidden.

Now Miss Rosie is gone, and buses loaded down with foreign tourists stop off at Little Zion to gawk at the headstone—one of three set down for Johnson in and around Greenwood—which rests in the wrong place in the right cemetery. I often drive down to meet groups and show them Miss Rosie's house, the church, and the spot where the 3 Forks stood. I talk about public records and the venereal-disease statistics of the Great Depression, but no one wants to hear it. They want to know about Johnson's life as heard through his eerily tuned guitar and the voice of a man who walked with hoodoo stones in his passway, side by side with the devil, just long enough to tell his tale. It's a good story, if not a true one.

Inscribed on the headstone is the image of a note in Johnson's hand, written as he lay dying and preserved by his sister. It reads, "Jesus of Nazareth King of Jerusalem, I know that my Redeemer liveth and that He will call me from the Grave."

HOW TO TALK FAULKNER

FOR THE EXPERIENCED and engaged reader, William Faulkner's prose isn't always confounding; sometimes it's incomprehensible. The genius of the South's great Nobel-winning modernist is evident in his prodigious imagination, mind-searing imagery, and his often gorgeous if challenging experimental style, particularly his use of multiple points of view, inimitable stream-of-consciousness exposition, and cadences with both rhythmic and disjunct effects. To the point: If you've never made page six of *The Sound and the Fury*, you're not alone.

Nevertheless, everyone should prepare for the inevitable cornering at a party by some half-drunk smart-ass who wants to know if you think *As I Lay Dying* is an ordinary family tragedy or a road-trip story bridging the gap between Homeric tradition and Hunter S. Thompson. In a truly Faulknerian sense, these confrontations are desirable; adversity determines the man. And when it comes to the master of Rowan Oak, you don't need a Ph.D. in literature or a loaded pistol to stand your ground, though either one will do in a pinch. What you need is a little context.

He was known as "Count No 'Count" by some neighbors, who sensed an air of superiority tempered by an air of being of no account. He was a precocious inebriate with a pathological aversion to air-conditioning. But Faulkner was also an artist, and as such he felt it was his job to reflect the world as it is. And he saw the world in his native Mississippi. To help us understand this world, Faulkner created the fictional Yoknapatawpha County, filled it with foolishly inclined aristocrats like the Sartoris family, and forced them to compete for space and oxygen with prolific hicks like the despicable Snopes clan of Frenchman's Bend. In the post–Civil War South, these tribes share a relationship similar to that of the dinosaurs and the egg-sucking rodents that took over following a certain meteor strike.

For some folks, reading Faulkner is both pleasurable and painful; it's also like bellying up to a twenty-four-hour all-you-care-to-eat buffet overflowing with decay, destruction, exploitation, murder, incest, suicide, mental dysfunction, and, of course, bears. That said, as culture critic H. L. Mencken once remarked, "this boy is a wonderful comedy writer." Faulkner's sometimes perverse sense of humor is especially helpful to remember when trapped in headier conversations about the unrepentantly difficult author. Because—like ol' Flem Snopes, who in *The Hamlet* raised the value of his worthless land by pretending to search for (nonexistent) gold—on some level, everybody's bluffing. Maybe even Faulkner.

SOUTHERN DIALECTS

FOLKS IN OTHER PARTS of the country might think that it's all just one slow drawl, but as anyone who has traveled from New Orleans to Tennessee can tell you, the so-called "Southern accent" is actually a collection of accents as different from one another as a beignet and a skillet of cornbread. Linguists identify a half dozen or more distinct ways of speaking in the South alone. And though we all speak a little bit differently, a few unique dialects stand out from the rest.

CAJUN ENGLISH: For generations, the Acadian inhabitants of Louisiana—known casually as Cajuns—spoke only French among one another. And though French is now in decline among the younger generations, the English spoken in the bayous of Louisiana remains fast, thickly accented, and peppered with French loanwords. It may not be a foreign language, but it can be nearly as difficult for outsiders to follow.

MOUNTAIN ENGLISH: The old myth that the dialects spoken in the Ozarks and Southern Appalachia are preserved forms of Shakespearean English is not entirely incorrect. Regional constructions like *a-going*, for example, are holdovers from the same antique English that gave us "afire" as a synonym for "on fire." But while the mountains did protect some older forms of speech, they also spawned a unique dialect heavily influenced by

Scotch-Irish immigrants and speckled with place-specific words such as "bald," meaning a summit with no trees, and "holler," or mountain valley. It is disappearing quickly these days due to an onslaught of outside influences.

OUTER BANKS BROGUE: British sailors settled the barrier islands of North Carolina in the early 1700s. Then, for more than two centuries, the water kept them mostly isolated from the mainland. The result? A dialect that sounds more like it belongs in the U.K. than the coastal South. Locals—nicknamed Hoi Toiders for their distinctive pronunciation of "high tide"—are sometimes mistaken for English or Irish tourists in other parts of the country.

SEA ISLAND CREOLE: Also known as Gullah or Geechee, this dialect is spoken by the African American inhabitants of the barrier islands around South Carolina and Georgia. Although it was dismissed for many years as broken English, linguists have shown that Sea Island Creole is, in fact, a mash-up of English and the African languages brought to the South by enslaved people centuries ago. Common words like *buckruh*, meaning "white man," and *cooter*, meaning "turtle"—the latter of which has spread into general usage in parts of the South—came to the Sea Islands from across the water.

YAT: If you hear what sounds like a Brooklyn accent on the streets of New Orleans, don't assume that you're listening to a Yankee. The Crescent City's "Yat" dialect—a swirl of French, Irish, German, and Italian inflections—can sound at times like Louisiana, at times like working-class New York, and at times like something all its own. The dialect takes its name from the phrase "Where y'at?," a New Orleans–style version of the more pedestrian "How's it going?"

MARDI GRAS LIKE A LOCAL

WE ALL HAVE an image of Mardi Gras: Teeming masses of sweaty, stumbling tourists in novelty hats making their way through Bourbon Street and drinking bright liquids from misshapen plastic containers. Girls baring their chests for beads. And something, God knows what, on the sidewalk that you are going to stay as far away from as humanly possible.

This is the TV version of Mardi Gras, and it does exist. It's worth seeing. Once. Not more than that. It's enough to turn most people off of the festival, New Orleans, and humanity in general. But in reality, it's only a very small piece of the party that is Carnival. This is a city-wide celebration, with endless pockets of debauchery and things to do that go far beyond the stereotypical image. Play your cards right, and you can learn New Orleans' best-kept secret: Mardi Gras isn't just for tourists. Here's how respectable locals do it.

The parade is the beating heart of Mardi Gras. It is the most visually impressive part of the celebration and the source of all beads. Before most parades hit the French Quarter, though, they take a long, leisurely trip through uptown via St. Charles Avenue. This is the best place to see them. Locals will go out early in the morning, or even the night before, to set up their stations. Find the right spot, grab a cooler of Abita, light up the grill, and settle in. Don't worry, you'll still get your beads.

Just because it's Mardi Gras doesn't mean that New Orleans isn't best enjoyed slow.

It used to be that the only people who paraded on Mardi Gras were those in ancient clubs with exclusive rolls and deep pockets, but that was a century ago. The ranks of krewes (who put on the parades and balls) have been exploding in recent years, and there's a whole lot of strange to see that goes way past Rex. It might be an entirely *Star Wars*–themed krewe or a tiny parade with six-inch floats. Mostly, this is a chance to see the amateur costumers of New Orleans on full display. If you're in town early, make your way to Krewe du Vieux and Krewe

Delusion three Saturdays before the big day. Otherwise, go to Box of Wine on the Sunday before, or St. Anne's on Fat Tuesday to witness strange people having a really good time. Or just grab a weird hat and join them.

At some point, you're going to venture into the madness that is the French Quarter, and you're going to have to find a way to keep vomit off of your shoes. See those people up above you, resting their drinks on wrought iron and gazing

down at the melee below? That's who you need to be. Call up old relatives, call up old friends' old relatives or just make new friends on the street—anything to get yourself a precious fifteen feet above the action. At that point, you can get a brief glimpse into a brilliantly aristocratic vision of an old-world festival. There are also balconies available for rent on Bourbon Street for an exorbitant price, but of course this is awful.

Once you've had your fill of the French Quarter, you might still feel the need to get stumbling drunk in a series of jazz clubs. This is where the Marigny comes in. The Marigny neighborhood is just downriver of the French Quarter—a little less dense, a little more residential, and a lot less disgusting. If you hit Frenchmen Street, you can get a glimpse of what Bourbon Street might have been before *Girls Gone Wild* and a series of corporate strip clubs beat whatever dirty

charm it might have once had clear out of it. This is where you can find the best music in the city and most of the locals who are out hitting the bars. You'll see only a hint of neon.

Finally, let's talk about coconuts. Most locals have enough beads. Even the flashing ones. After you've spent one year gathering bag after bag of useless, beer-soaked plastic spheres, you've sort of had your fill. But the special throws, those are something else. Locals lust after glittery coconuts from Zulu, feathered shoes from Muses, or the occasional pack of glass beads that harkens back to a time before the endless ocean of Chinese imports. Some people have collections of unique "doubloons" that go back decades. The best way to get good throws is to be a five-year-old child, but everyone else has to get right up to the float and find a way to get noticed. It won't be easy, but it will be fun.

INSTRUCTIONS IN THE BLUES

TO WRITE A BLUES these days, it seems, the first thing you absolutely must do is buy a hat. It can be a felt trilby, a straw porkpie, a classic ivy, or even a colorful beret. Once you acquire a nice Hawaiian shirt to match the new lid, you're more than halfway there.

Now, let's consider form. It's called "12-bar" blues for a reason. If you want to wake up in the morning full of mournful regret, it's best to pitch your nightly wang-dang-doodles in as many bars as possible, then eat a pork chop at three o'clock in the a.m. Consciousness is key here, because later you'll want to brag about how good it was, tell everyone how it browned your sweet, sweet gravy. Mingle your thoughts about chops and gravy and your supreme desirability among all the world's women with explosive onomatopoeia, e.g., *bang* or *boom*. Toss in a "baby" where appropriate, and set it to any old beat. When you've got it, apparently, the blues is what you say it is.

But isn't that all a little too easy? Will your rider tap her foot and say, "Mmm-hmmm"? Quite possibly not. Likewise, mere virtuosity is as common as gravy stains on a Hawaiian shirt, and if that thought leaves you too depressed to even express the blues, you may be one of those rare few who can't be satisfied with the twenty-first-century Beale Street standard. If you indeed seek to emulate the pre-hat greats—or at least honor and build on their foundation—get out of the bars and onto the back porch. Pick up a cigar-box guitar, a jug, a banjo, a washtub bass, or a fiddle—something that depends on the human body for every sound it makes. Sit down at an upright piano, bite a harmonica, wear a washboard, or just clap your hands and sing. And remind yourself, as you work steadily through the same three chords over and over again, that the blues ain't about hoodoo or squeezing as many notes as possible into a dozen bars. It's about little truths, tall tall tales, and all the sweet, languorous silences in between.

THE BRILLIANCE OF SOUTHERN FOLK ART

BY ACE ATKINS AND ANGELA MOORE ATKINS

ALTHOUGH HER WORK hangs in the Museum of Modern Art, in New York, most people outside the South have never heard of Theora Hamblett. Born in Paris, Mississippi, and largely self-taught, the former schoolteacher began painting in her fifties, depicting scenes from her childhood. Those images tell stories about everyday rural life and the natural world through her shimmering, pointillist trees and folk-style landscapes.

Then she started painting her dreams and visions.

An artistic eccentric, Hamblett was also a Southern Baptist who saw heaven at work on earth as clearly as Warhol saw soup cans. An Oxford local once ran into Hamblett at the grocery store, standing stock-still, staring at a soup-can display.

"Jesus is there," she said. Sure enough, if you squinted a little and made your vision fuzzy, you could begin to see the outlines of what might be an image of the savior. But she saw Him in Technicolor, and that's what she painted—golden chariots and angels and silver stairways to heaven.

She and others like her recorded a life now lost to modernity. Fascinated by the natural and supernatural worlds, they're often called "folk" artists or "outsider" artists, and when people think of their work, if they think of it at all, they may recall a rural scene painted in a childlike manner and think it's charming, in a condescending way, perhaps calling it "cute" or "quaint." The irony is that such notions are themselves quaint, not to mention myopic. Though often under-recognized or unknown, the South's great "folk" artists transcend idioms and stand out as visionaries peculiar to our region.

Louisiana painter Clementine Hunter was also self-taught: Once she had the tools, art poured out of her. Hunter was the granddaughter of a slave, and like her forebears, she was born, lived, and worked on a plantation until her death at the age of 101. Like Hamblett, she began painting in her fifties, after the owner of the plantation where she lived began inviting artists to visit and work there; they encouraged her natural talent. She painted scenes of African American plantation life from memory: baptisms, picking cotton, and nature. The Ogden Museum of Southern Art, in New Orleans, has scores of her paintings in its collection. (A new wing of its library is named in her honor.) Her work is raw and often maximalist and surreal, forgoing the limitations of the world as observed. It can evoke work by the American modernist Marsden Hartley and the German expressionist Max Beckmann.

Mississippian Walter Anderson came from privilege but shared Hunter's drive to create art on anything: paper, pottery, walls, linoleum printing blocks. His gorgeous, masterly watercolors of the Mississippi Gulf Coast's natural splendor are at once impressionism and augmented reality, such is their intensity, yet Anderson is still a relative unknown in America.

"He created because he needed to," says Ligia Römer, of the Walter Anderson Museum of Art, in Ocean Springs. "He wasn't trying to change the art world. He wanted to make the beauty of nature accessible to everyone."

Anderson would disappear for days at a time, following a flock of pelicans through marshland or rowing a canoe to uninhabited Horn Island and creating like a wild man. During 1965's Hurricane Betsy, he tied himself to a tree to experience the storm. Hurricanes would become a theme: Anderson's family property, where much of his work remained, flooded during Hurricane Katrina, and many paintings were damaged or lost. A recent exhibition of his watercolors featured some still streaked with Mississippi mud, Römer says. She suspects he would've thought them more beautiful.

Arkansas artist Carroll Cloar shared Hamblett's sense of "Southern gothic," says Stanton Thomas, a curator at the Memphis Brooks Museum of Art. Cloar, a classically trained artist, painted magical-realist scenes of the Delta of his childhood. But he never enjoyed widespread critical acceptance.

"Really, Cloar is an incredibly complicated artist whose images are, on the surface, very lyrical," Thomas says. And though Cloar showed in New York, the major gallerists ignored his deeper meaning and symbolism.

It's a mistake the art world has often made regarding Southern artists.

Statesville, North Carolina's McKendree Long was a classmate of Georgia O'Keeffe's. As a young man, Long studied under famed Hungarian portraitist Philip de László in Europe, but a *New York Times* review of an exhibition of his work proclaimed it "zany." Long's apocalyptic images, inspired by the Book of Revelation, are dense, but for anyone familiar with evangelical Protestantism and cultural history, his paintings are firmly rooted in theology, reminiscent of the work of two great old-world masters: Hieronymus Bosch and Albrecht Dürer.

Brad Thomas, a curator at Charlotte's Mint Museum, organized a Long retrospective in 2002. He says the fine-art student turned fire-and-brimstone Baptist preacher came back to art late in his life, as the cultural tumult of the fifties, sixties, and seventies raged around him. "Reverend Long is stamping his feet and shaking his fist in his paintings," Thomas says. "He was compelled by faith, compelled by his religious convictions. His artistic talent merged with his religion, and all hell broke loose on the canvas."

Many Southerners find Long's apocalypse familiar, including scholars William Ferris and Charles Reagan Wilson. It's an old story we've heard many times before. We wouldn't call it zany. Cloar's magical realism and regular old realism are brilliant, sometimes haunting, and often hilarious. Hunter's and Hamblett's paintings of rural Southern life are visual representations of our grandmothers' stories and spiritual convictions, pure and true. Anderson's wild naturalism is our backyard living and breathing with a supernatural vibrancy we would do well to remember.

The South's greatest artists aren't "outsiders." They're us.

MAKE A DIDDLEY BOW

EVERY ONCE IN a while, you find your-self in need of a musical instrument. Maybe you only have a board, some nails, and a tin can or an old glass bottle. Per-fect. That's plenty to cobble together a diddley bow.

West African slaves brought a version of the diddley bow, a one-stringed slide guitar, to the Mississippi Delta centuries ago. For years, Delta bluesmen kept it alive as a children's toy, a way to work teenagers up to the six-string guitar. But children's toy or not, the diddley bow can wail in the right hands. It has no frets or tuning pegs; all you need to play it are a slide—glass or metal—and a feel for the blues.

Traditionally, one strings a diddley bow with broom wire, the heavy stuff that holds a straw broom head to its handle. If you don't have an old broom handy, buy a coil of music wire. Or, for a shorter did-dley bow, try a guitar string.

Before you begin building your instru-ment, don a pair of protective glasses, to avoid injury from a snapped string or a shattered bottle. Then, cut a board to about three feet in length, or grab any lap-length piece of wood lying around the house. Hammer two sturdy nails on opposite ends of the board, about an inch from each end.

Wrap the wire around one of the nails a few times—and then around itself—to keep it from slipping. Do the same on the other nail, keeping the wire tight. Then, slip a tin can or a sturdy, nontapered glass bottle under the wire, pushing it as close to one of the nails as it will go. Pull it out, use a rasp to wear a light indentation into the spot where it will sit, and push it back into place. Then, slip a small block of scrap wood as close to the other nail as possible.

Block situated, pluck the string. It should resonate. If it doesn't, the wire needs more tension. Tighten the wire or insert a taller block of wood. Finally, when the string is humming, pour a glass of your beverage of choice, set the diddley bow on your lap, and take up your slide. Pick the string near the bottle or can while working your slide up and down the other end. Let the blues roll out.

THE GREAT SOUTHERN NOVEL

BY DANIEL WALLACE

I DON'T KNOW HOW to write the Great Southern Novel, and even if I did I wouldn't be saying. I'd keep it a secret and get busy. I'd write it myself, and then I'd probably write another. Why stop at one? Who knows how many I could write? Chances are I'd stop at three, because a trilogy of Great Southern Novels would be a tolerable contribution to the literature, whereas a quartet would be overmuch, a surfeit, more like bragging about how I know how to write the Great Southern Novel.

But I don't know how to write it, and neither do you. There have been some good ones, even great ones—think Faulkner's *Light in August*, Walker Percy's *The Moviegoer*, Harper Lee's *To Kill a Mockingbird*, et cetera—just not *the* great one.

I don't even think the Great Southern Novel *can* be written. It has to be discovered. I think you have to be more than a writer to write a great book; you have to be an adventurer. To me, it's as if the book already exists, somewhere between lower West Virginia and New Orleans, and we have to find it.

That's why we can talk about the existence of a *Southern* novel at all, and why the South can claim the only truly distinct American literature defined by geography. Faulkner had just his "little postage stamp of native soil," and the South takes up a big swath of this country, so there's a lot of room left to roam.

Writers are explorers, and each of us has our own secret map leading to the treasure. We study this map all of our writing lives, and by the time we're done with it, it's as fragile as ash, crumbling at the edges, hieroglyphic, unreadable. But we hold on to it; we *believe* in it. It's belief in this map that keeps a writer writing—for years, sometimes decades—before finding what feels like the right place to dig. You may be the only one who believes in your map's veracity; there will be people out there who think you're a fool for following it, because the chances that you'll strike gold are slim to none. But that's not what it's about. It's about the things you find along the way, amazing things: stories covered in moss, essays torn and caked in mud, even a few wonderful novels sometimes, scattered like fool's gold. In this way a lot of great books have been discovered, just not *the* great book. These books we have found are the clues that something greater is out there. We haven't found it yet because we'll never find it. But we keep digging.

Hole after hole, deeper and deeper and deeper. We know something is down there, and it's just a little farther south, and it's Great.

Because the Great Southern Novel exists already, buried deep in the ground—somewhere in the side of an Indian mound, beneath your granddaddy's rickety old barn, lost in the swampy muck of some spooky bayou . . .

It's why our authors write about the *land* so much: They're all out there on it, in it, looking for this novel. Harper Lee had a shovel and surprising upper-body strength. She dug as long as she could and came out with something shiny. Walker Percy, tubercular, had to hire a crew. And Faulkner was out there on his particular postage stamp with a mule and a sod buster almost every weekend. And so many more like them, too many to name—they weren't, still aren't, afraid to get their hands dirty.

★

ACKNOWLEDGMENTS

A book of this scope is the work of a small army. And to lead the charge, you need an adept and agile project editor. Thankfully, Jeremy Spencer stepped up to the task. He corralled a great group of talented writers, kept everyone on track, and saw the book through to the end. Around the *Garden & Gun* offices, just about everyone pitched in with advice, wisdom, and work. Deputy Editor David Mezz fine-tuned the entire manuscript, and Editorial Assistant Jed Portman uncovered experts in every category, from rope throwing to the art of mixing a proper drink with absinthe. Both made this a better book, and I'm extremely grateful for their dedication. Art Director Marshall McKinney and Assistant Art Director Braxton Crim contributed to the design of the book and the illustrations. As for the illustrations: It was a delight and an honor to land the wildly accomplished Bruce Hutchison as the book's illustrator. Copy Chief Donna Levine brought the same intensity to this project that she brings to every piece of copy that runs in the magazine. Knowing her eyes were focused on the manuscript helped me rest easy at night. And, last but not least, thanks to all the writers, many of whom are regulars in the pages of *G&G*, who contributed to this book. Their passion and voice are evident on every page.

The magazine's literary agent, the talented Amy Hughes of the Dunow, Carlson, & Lerner Literary Agency, found a suitable home for this book with HarperWave. There Karen Rinaldi and Julie Will brought our vision to reality with a deft touch, also managing the nearly impossible task of keeping us on schedule, while challenging us to raise the bar at every point.

Finally, huge kudos to the owners of *Garden & Gun*, Rebecca Wesson Darwin, Pierre Manigault, and J. Edward Bell III. When the teeth of the recession were grinding magazines of all sizes into a paste, these three stood by a small start-up that has grown into something beyond what many of us could have dreamed of.

ABOUT THE CONTRIBUTORS

ACE ATKINS is the *New York Times* bestselling author of more than a dozen novels, including the forthcoming *The Broken Places*. A native of Alabama, Atkins once played SEC football and was nominated for a Pulitzer Prize on the newspaper-crime beat. He and his family and many animals live on an old farm outside Oxford, Mississippi.

ANGELA MOORE ATKINS is a native of North Carolina with a master's in Southern studies from Ole Miss. She's been a crime reporter, a PR hack, an advertising copywriter, a community-magazine editor, and a contributor to *The New Encyclopedia of Southern Culture*. She lives on a century-old farm outside Oxford, Mississippi, with her husband, the novelist Ace Atkins.

ROY BLOUNT, JR., is the author of twenty-three books, including *Alphabetter Juice: The Joy of Text* and *Long Time Leaving: Dispatches from Up South*. He is a *Garden & Gun* columnist, a panelist on *Wait . . . Wait, Don't Tell Me*, and a member of the Fellowship of Southern Authors.

DOMINIQUE BROWNING is the author of several books, most recently *Slow Love: How I Lost My Job, Put on My Pajamas, and Found Happiness*; she blogs at slow lovelife.com. She is the cofounder and senior director of Moms Clean Air Force, a special project of the Environmental Defense Fund. She was previously the editor in chief of Condé Nast's *House & Garden*; her magazine career includes positions at *Newsweek*, *Texas Monthly*, and *Esquire*.

MONTE BURKE is a staff writer at *Forbes*. He is the author of the books *4th and Goal* and *Sowbelly*.

JOHN CURRENCE, a chef born and raised in New Orleans, now presides over Oxford, Mississippi's City Grocery Group and its four critically acclaimed restaurants. Winner of the 2009 James Beard Foundation Award for Best Chef, South, Currence is also an avid outdoorsman and a contributing editor for *Garden & Gun*.

CHRIS DAVIS lives in Memphis with his wife, Charlotte; their twins, Josie and Lucy; two cats; and the ghost of Nathan Bedford Forrest. He has written for *Details*, once posed topless for *Maxim*, and is a longtime staff writer for *The Memphis Flyer*, among many other things. He also sings and plays guitar for the country band Papa Top's West Coast Turnaround.

DAVID DiBENEDETTO is the editor in chief of *Garden & Gun*, where he oversees all media platforms. He's also the author of *On the Run: An Angler's Journey Down the Striper Coast*.

CHRIS DIXON is a former editor of *Surfer* magazine and the author of *Ghost Wave: The Discovery of Cortes Bank and the Biggest Wave on Earth*. He has written for *Garden & Gun*, the *New York Times*, *Outside*, *Men's Journal*, and others. He lives in Charleston, South Carolina, with his family.

JOHN T. EDGE is the director of the Center for the Study of Southern Culture, at the University of Mississippi, and a contributing editor for *Garden & Gun*.

HAL ESPEN is a former senior editor at the *New Yorker* and former editor in chief of *Outside*. He worships at the Bar-B-Q Shop in Memphis, blogs at stoneturntable .net, and has written for the *New York Times*, the *Atlantic*, the *Los Angeles Times*, and many other publications.

JENNY EVERETT is a freelance writer and editor based in Charleston, South Carolina. She writes the "What's in Season" column for *Garden & Gun*.

ALLISON GLOCK is the author of the *New York Times* Notable Book and Whiting Award–winning *Beauty before Comfort*. Her work has been published in the *New York Times*; *GQ*; *Rolling Stone*; *Esquire*; the *New York Times Magazine*; the *New Yorker*; *O, The Oprah Magazine*; *Elle*; *Marie Claire*; and many others. She is a contributing editor for *Garden & Gun*, a senior writer at ESPN, a columnist for *Southern Living*, and the recipient of a GLAAD award. Her first poem was recently published in the *New Yorker*. She is the co-author of *Changers*.

ALEX HEARD, a native of Jackson, Mississippi, has written and edited for numerous publications, including the *New Republic*, the *New York Times Magazine*, *Spy*, *Wired*, and *Outside*, where he works as editorial director. He's also the author of *The Eyes of Willie McGee* and *Apocalypse Pretty Soon*.

ROBERT HICKS, the author of the *New York Times* bestsellers *The Widow of the South* and *A Separate Country*, is also an essayist, a preservationist, a community activist, a gardener, and the "curator of vibe" for the B.B. King Blues Clubs.

JACK HITT is a contributing writer to the *New York Times Magazine* as well as a contributor to *Garden & Gun*. His book *Off the Road: A Modern-Day Walk Down the Pilgrim's Route into Spain* was made into a 2012 motion picture, *The Way*, directed by Emilio Estevez and starring Martin Sheen. He has won the Livingston and Pope Awards, and, most recently, his *Harper's* report on American anthropology was selected for a collection of the best science writing of the past twenty-five years, *The Best of the Best of American Science Writing*. His work also appears in the *New Yorker*, *Harper's*, *Rolling Stone*, and *Wired*. His one-man show, *Making Up the Truth*, ran at the Public Theater in New York in

November 2012. A paperback of his book *Bunch of Amateurs: A Search for the American Character* came out in May 2013.

ELIZABETH HUTCHISON was raised in Charleston, South Carolina, where she split summers between the beaches near her parents' home and her grandparents' upstate peach farm, where her grandmother, a former librarian, instilled in her a love of the written word. A graduate of Clemson University, she is an editorial assistant at *Garden & Gun*.

PABLEAUX JOHNSON is a writer and photographer based in New Orleans. He is also the author of three books on Louisiana food culture and the founder of the electronic publishing company Blue Crab Labs. Johnson has pronounced weaknesses for thick-sliced bacon, fine bourbon whiskey, funky sousaphones, raw oysters, coconut cream pie, and talking-dog jokes.

JOHN KESSLER is the chief dining writer at the *Atlanta Journal-Constitution*. His work has been anthologized in *Best Food Writing* eight times, and he serves on the journalism committee for the James Beard Awards.

FRANCINE MAROUKIAN is a two-time James Beard Foundation Award winner and a contributor at *Esquire*, where her work earned the 2009 ASME National Magazine Award in the "Leisure Interests" category.

GUY MARTIN, an Alabama native, is a contributing editor for *Garden & Gun* and *Condé Nast Traveler*. He has written for many other publications as well, including *Wired* (UK), the (Sunday) *London Telegraph*, the *London Observer*, and the *New Yorker*. He writes about the South and about Eastern Europe, where he is at work on a book about the Cold War in Berlin. He lives in New York City, Alabama, and Berlin, spending much of his time on the many different airplanes that fly between them.

DAVID MEZZ was born in Chapel Hill, North Carolina, and is the deputy editor of *Garden & Gun*. An avid fisherman, he lives in Charleston, South Carolina, and is known for his surgical precision with a fillet knife.

JONATHAN MILES is the author of *Dear American Airlines*, which was named a *New York Times* Notable Book and a Best Book of 2008 by the *Wall Street Journal* and the *Los Angeles Times*. He is a former columnist for the *New York Times*, and his journalism, essays, and literary criticism have appeared in the *New York Times Book Review*, *GQ*, *Details*, *Men's Journal*, the *New York Observer*, *Field & Stream*, *Outside*, *Garden & Gun*, *Food & Wine*, and many other magazines. His work has been included numerous times in the annual *Best American Sports Writing* and *Best American Crime Writing* anthologies. A former longtime resident of Oxford, Mississippi, he currently lives in New Jersey. His latest novel is *Want Not*.

JESSICA MISCHNER is a senior editor at *Garden & Gun*. When she's not chasing story leads or the next class of Made in the South Award winners, she enjoys collecting julep cups with other people's monograms, perfecting the art of the bacon cracker, and spending time with her husband, Will, and son, Camp.

ROBERT MOSS is a food writer and culinary historian based in Charleston, South Carolina. His books include *Barbecue: The History of an American Institution* and *Going Lardcore: Adventures in New Southern Dining*.

T. EDWARD NICKENS, editor at large of *Field & Stream* and a contributing editor of *Audubon*, fell in love with duck hunting in the beaver swamps of North Carolina's Piedmont region. He's traveled and written about waterfowling from the Northwest Territories to the tip of Atchafalaya Bay.

DAVID E. PETZAL, the rifles field editor of *Field & Stream*, has been with the publication since 1972. A graduate of Colgate University, he served in the U.S. Army from 1963 to 1969, and he began writing about rifles and rifle shooting during his service in 1964. He has hunted all over the United States and Canada, as well as in Europe, Africa, and New Zealand. In 2002 he was awarded the Leupold Jack Slack Writer of the Year Award, and in 2005 he received the Zeiss Outdoor Writer of the Year Award, making him the first person to win both.

JED PORTMAN is an editorial assistant at *Garden & Gun*. He got his first taste of good barbecue at the Georgia Pig, just off I-95 in Brunswick, Georgia. Though the Pig is no more, the Charleston, South Carolina–based Portman's passion for smoke, grease, and rickety roadside restaurants lives on.

M. K. QUINLAN grew up in Birmingham, Alabama, and was raised to have an equal passion for football and the finer things in life, which has served her well in her role as style editor at *Garden & Gun*. A graduate of Georgetown University, she trained as an interior designer in Washington, D.C.

HANNA RASKIN is a food writer and restaurant critic. Her work has appeared in *Garden & Gun*, *Southern Living*, and *Cooking Light*, and she has served as the food critic for *Seattle Weekly*, the *Dallas Observer*, and Asheville, North Carolina's *Mountain Xpress*.

JULIA REED is a contributing editor for *Garden & Gun*, where she writes the magazine's "The High & The Low" column. She is the author of *But Mama Always Put Vodka in Her Sangria*; *Ham Biscuits, Hostess Gowns, and Other Southern Specialties*; *Queen of the Turtle Derby and Other Southern Phenomena*; and *The House on First Street: My New Orleans Story*.

NATALIE ERMANN RUSSELL is a writer and editor based in Charlottesville, Virginia. She edits the local-foods magazine *Edible Blue Ridge* and never refuses an invitation to spend the day at a nearby farm. Sometimes she has to be told it's time to go home.

JEREMY K. SPENCER is a writer and editor from Memphis, Tennessee.

BRYS STEPHENS is a food writer based in Charleston, South Carolina. He is currently working on his first cookbook.

DAVID THIER is a writer based in New Orleans. His work has appeared in *Garden & Gun*, the *New York Times*, and *Forbes*.

DANIEL WALLACE lives in Chapel Hill, North Carolina, where he directs the creative-writing program at UNC. He's the author of five novels, most recently *The Kings and Queens of Roam.* His first book, *Big Fish*, has been translated into twenty-five languages and was made into a movie and a Broadway musical.

DONOVAN WEBSTER is the author of nine books and has written for the *New Yorker, Vanity Fair, National Geographic, Smithsonian,* the *New York Times Magazine,* and others. An avid trout fisherman and reluctant screenwriter, he lives with his wife and children in the country outside Charlottesville, Virginia, and in Santa Fe, New Mexico.

INDEX

ABOUT

GARDEN&GUN

MAGAZINE

Garden & Gun is a national magazine that covers the best of the South, including its sporting culture, food, music, art, and literature, and its people and their ideas. The magazine has won numerous awards for journalism, design, and overall excellence. *Garden & Gun* was launched in the spring of 2007 and is head-quartered in Charleston, South Carolina.